Springer Texts in Business and Economics

Springer Texts in Business and Economics (STBE) delivers high-quality instructional content for undergraduates and graduates in all areas of Business/Management Science and Economics. The series is comprised of self-contained books with a broad and comprehensive coverage that are suitable for class as well as for individual self-study. All texts are authored by established experts in their fields and offer a solid methodological background, often accompanied by problems and exercises.

Diwakar Gupta

Healthcare Analytics

An Operations Perspective

Springer

Diwakar Gupta
The University of Texas at Austin
Austin, TX, USA

ISSN 2192-4333 ISSN 2192-4341 (electronic)
Springer Texts in Business and Economics
ISBN 978-3-032-24834-3 ISBN 978-3-032-24835-0 (eBook)
https://doi.org/10.1007/978-3-032-24835-0

This Springer imprint is published by the registered company Springer Nature Switzerland AG
The registered company address is: Gewerbestrasse 11, 6330 Cham, Switzerland

Preface

About This Book

This book is about the US healthcare system. No attempt is made to describe health systems in other countries. It focuses on real-world challenges faced by operations managers in clinical settings, such as optimizing capacity, patient flow, staffing, scheduling, and revenue. The ideas presented in this book are based on the context and data that the author encountered when working with healthcare clinics and hospitals. Some of these experiences have been written up as short cases that are accompanied by data. Data have been de-identified and names of all organizations and actors are fictitious. However, the context is real.

Designed for advanced undergraduates and professional master's program students with no prior knowledge of the US healthcare system, the book features in-class and at-home exercises, as well as multiple-choice questions to reinforce learning. Several functions in R are used throughout the book, e.g., *qnorm* and *pnorm* for normal distribution without explaining what they mean. Adopting instructors may consider a short tutorial on R functions at the start of the class. The supporting materials include data sets that go with the short cases based on the author's consulting experience. R script files and case-analysis slides are available to adopting instructors.

The book is written in a conversational style. It is presented in a modular format that allows instructors to tailor content to their students' needs, including options to omit technical sections or delve into three technical notes for those with a stronger mathematical background.

Copyright and License

School of Business are granted a limited-term and limited-use license to use this book while they are registered in the classes for the purpose of enhancing their learning. Students are also granted access to the data used in the case studies.

Austin, TX, USA Diwakar Gupta

Competing Interests The author has no competing interests to declare that are relevant to the content of this manuscript.

Contents

List of Figures

List of Tables

List of Abbreviations

ACO	Accountable Care Organization. 72
ALOS	Average Length of Stay. 64
BEA	Bureau of Economic Analysis https://www.bea.gov/data/gdp/gdp-industry. 11
CMS	Centers for Medicare and Medicaid Services (https://www.cms.gov/). 6, 8
CPT	Current Procedural Terminology. 15, 18, 39
ED	Emergency Department. 63
FFS	Fee for Service – a payment paradigm in which the health care provider is paid for each service rendered. 6, 12, 39
HUC	Health Unit Coordinator. 63
IPPS	The Inpatient Prospective Payment System – a system of paying hospitals by patient DRG at discharge, irrespective of the length of stay and services rendered. 65
LOS	Length of Stay. 64
MA	Medical Assistant. 21, 22, 43
MD	Medical Doctor. 21, 39
NP	Nurse Practitioner. 24, 39
OECD	Organization for Economic Co-operation and Development. 4, 5
OR	Operating Room. 63
QALY	The quality-adjusted life-year (QALY) combines the length of life and the quality of life into a single index number. It is a measure of change in utility induced by the treatment multiplied by the duration of the treatment effect. 11
RN	Registered Nurse. 22
ToD	Time of Day. 67
USG	The US Federal Government. 3, 4, 6, 9

Part I
The Basics

Chapter 1
The US Healthcare System

1.1 Introduction

A healthcare system typically consists of:

1. Regulatory agencies
2. Payers/insurers
3. Institutional service providers
4. Healthcare professionals (providers)
5. Patients

Different countries have different systems for paying, provisioning, and regulating healthcare delivery. Some countries have instituted universal health insurance that covers a certain level of healthcare services for all citizens and legal residents. State and federal tax revenues are used to pay for the healthcare expenditures. Beneficiaries may be asked to contribute to the national plan and may have options available to purchase additional coverage. Many countries have built state-run hospitals and clinics that provide direct care to members of the public. Most countries have a mixture of public and private provision of health insurance and healthcare services. Nearly all have laws, regulations, and licensure requirements governing the conduct of institutions and health professionals that provide healthcare services.

In the USA, health insurance for most people is tied to their employment. It is provided by employers as an employment benefit. The US government (USG) provides insurance for older adults (>65 years of age) through its Medicare[1] program, and for certain disadvantaged populations through its Medicaid[2] program.

[1] See https://www.medicare.gov/what-medicare-covers/your-medicare-coverage-choices/whats-medicare for a quick introduction.

[2] A side-by-side comparison of the Medicare and Medicaid programs can be found at https://www.cms.gov/Outreach-and-Education/Medicare-Learning-Network-MLN/MLNProducts/Downloads/ProgramBasics.pdf.

D. Gupta, *Healthcare Analytics*, Springer Texts in Business and Economics,
https://doi.org/10.1007/978-3-032-24835-0_1

According to the US Census Bureau (https://www.census.gov/library/publications/2021/demo/p60-274.html) in 2020, 8.6% of people, or 28.0 million, did not have health insurance at some point during the year. In 2020, private versus public coverage percentages were 66.5 percent and 34.8 percent, respectively. Of the subcategories of health insurance coverage, employment-based insurance was the most common, covering 54.4 percent of the population for some or all of the calendar year, followed by Medicare (18.4 percent), Medicaid (17.8 percent), direct-purchase coverage (10.5 percent), TRICARE[3] (2.8 percent), and Department of Veterans Affairs (VA) or Civilian Health and Medical Program of the Department of Veterans Affairs (CHAMPVA) coverage (0.9 percent). The vast majority of healthcare services are provided by private (either for profit or not for profit) entities. Notable exceptions are healthcare facilities operated by the Department of Veterans Affairs (for veterans) and the Department of Defense (for active-duty military personnel).

There is a subtle distinction between payers and insurers, which may be explained as follows. Insurers typically charge a premium, which may be paid either by individuals in a direct-purchase arrangement, or by a combination of employers and individuals, in return for a particular level of benefits via their health insurance plans. In some situations, insurers carry the risk associated with actual expenditures exceeding the monies they collect via premiums. In these cases, they are also the payers. In contrast, many large employers are self-insured, which makes them the payers. Although the contracted insurance company collects insurance premiums from their employees, the employers pay actual expenditures and bear the risk of expenditures exceeding their budgets plus the total premiums collected. In such cases, insurance companies serve as adjudicators of claims and as entities that use their market power to negotiate prices with providers. Finally, uninsured individuals bear financial risk and pay all costs on an out-of-pocket basis, which makes them payers. Notwithstanding the distinction between payers and insurers, and whether the insurer is the USG, or employers, or individuals, eventually all payments come from the beneficiaries of healthcare services—either through direct payment of insurance premiums, or lower pay in lieu of healthcare coverage, or taxes, or some combination of these.

1.2 USA Versus Other Developed Countries

Let us compare how the USA stacks up against other OECD countries. We begin by comparing expenditures. Reported expenditures data by country may be downloaded from the OECD website by specifying the country, the year, and the type of expenses. In fact, the OECD website provides a handy tool to plot the trends.

[3] Tricare is a healthcare program for uniformed service members.

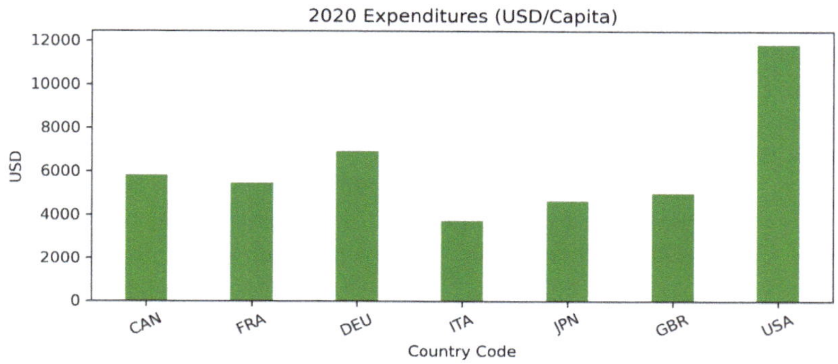

Fig. 1.1 G7 Health Expenditures 2020 Statistics. *Note:* The G7 countries are Canada, France, Germany, Italy, Japan, Great Britain, and USA

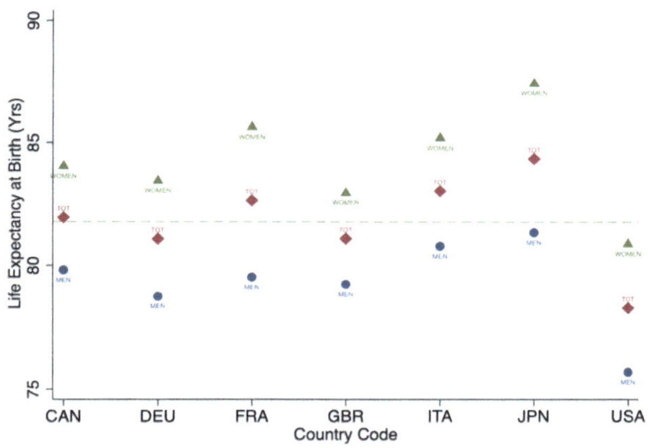

Fig. 1.2 Life expectancy at birth (latest data). TOT = total of men and women

In what follows, the 2020 data (latest available at the time of writing this book) were used to generate a bar chart. Reported expenditures are in USD. Clearly, US expenditures far exceed those of other developed countries. Let us next examine some aggregate measures of outcomes. A simple, flawed, but commonly used measure of overall health outcomes is the average life expectancy at birth. Similar to Fig. 1.1, data were obtained from the OECD website for the same seven countries for which the expenditures were calculated. These data are plotted in Fig. 1.2.

We observe that while the USA has the largest per capital expenditures, its life expectancy at birth is the lowest among the G7 countries. At least on this simple aggregate metric, healthcare in the USA is not as effective as in other developed countries. There are many reasons for this. Some of these reasons, e.g., income inequality, lack of educational opportunities, a more heterogeneous population mix, and a greater willingness to utilize more expensive technologies without commensurately higher benefit, are beyond the scope of this book. However, one of the reasons is not, and that is *waste*. In fact, it has been estimated that in 2017 the annual waste in US health spending might have been as high as $750 billion (approximately $2300 per person).

Why is waste so pervasive? To understand the reasons and to develop effective strategies for improving resource utilization, managers need to become familiar with the complicated processes and the combination of people, systems, and technologies that produce healthcare. Effective resource utilization in healthcare depends on careful matching of supply and demand in a highly random and human environment. Prevalent approaches used to pay for health services may induce self-interested actors involved in the production of health services to take actions that produce waste. For example, the fee for service (FFS) payment mechanism induces providers to prioritize volume of offered services even when they may be medically unnecessary, redundant, or ineffective.

Managers must also become familiar with what data are usually available and how to apply advanced analytic methods to improve operations, while maintaining focus on health outcomes and patient experience. For example, while on the one hand, inadequate physician staffing at an Emergency Department can lead to long wait times, adverse health outcomes, and even death, on the other hand, too much capacity is wasteful although it may reduce wait times. What is the right balance? Managers attempting to address such issues must also be familiar with laws such as the Emergency Medical Treatment and Labor Act, and local regulations that limit a hospital's ability to turn away patients arriving via ambulance. The ideas presented in this book will help students learn how people, systems, and data are connected in the delivery of healthcare and how to use data and analytic methods to answer questions that confront healthcare operations managers daily.

Because the majority of the people in the USA receive their health coverage from their employers, there is often a misconception that in the USA the majority of healthcare spending is private spending. The reality is different, as shown in Fig. 1.3 prepared by CMS, Office of the Actuary, National Health Statistics Group.

In fact, using Fig. 1.3, one may calculate the total government expenditures as follows:

- Insurance: $(0.73)*(0.70) = 0.511$.
- Public health: 0.03.
- Investment (e.g., NIH): 0.05.
- Total government expenditures $= 0.591$ or $\approx 59\%$.
- Therefore, total nongovernmental expenditures $= 41\%$.

That is, the majority of the expenditures are incurred by federal and state governments. The reason why we observe this pattern is that the USG is responsible for healthcare costs of the most expensive segments of the population—those over 65, and those with limited income or disability, and children. Still, about 28 million people (8.6%) in the USA had no health insurance in 2020. Some may argue that

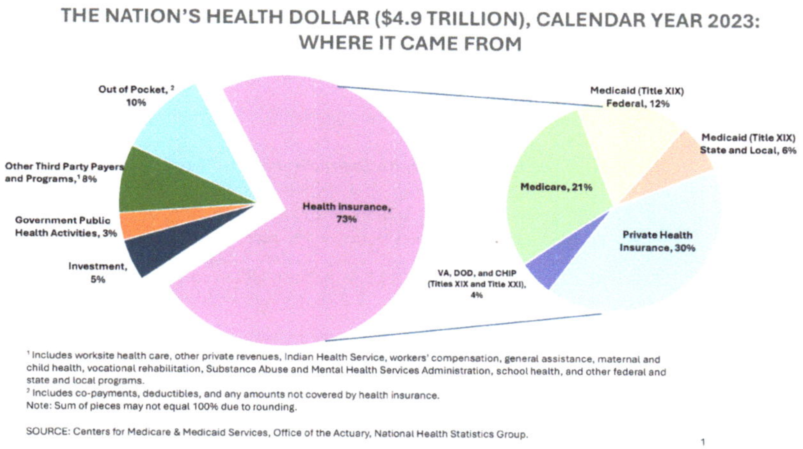

Fig. 1.3 Who pays for US health expenditures

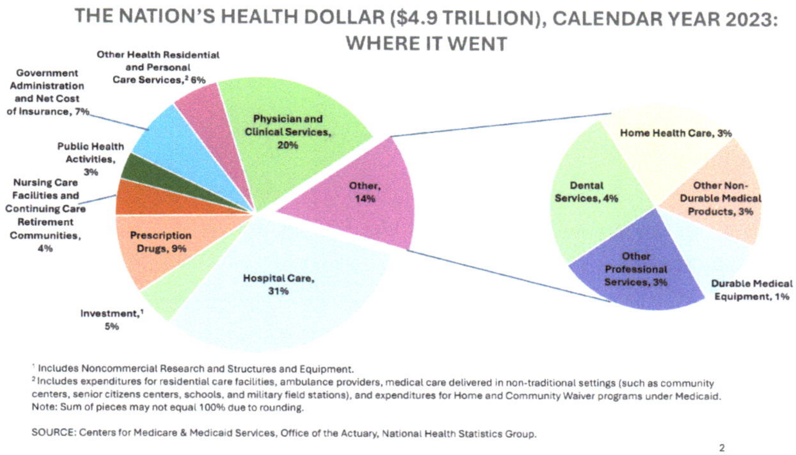

Fig. 1.4 How the US healthcare dollars are spent

all expenses are eventually paid by the people, either in the form of taxes or direct payment to insurers and providers. Therefore, the distinction between government and nongovernment expenses should be irrelevant. While it is true that all expenses are eventually paid by the people, the distinction still matters because government expenditures are involuntary, whereas private expenditures are usually voluntary. An exhibit similar to Fig. 1.3 (see Fig. 1.4) shows how the healthcare dollars are spent.

Note that the largest expense category is hospital care, followed by physician and clinical services. Hospital care is typically for acute care episodes. In relative terms, the US spends less on primary and preventative care. This may be responsible, in part, for relatively worse health outcomes. Exhibit 1 shows how national expenditures have grown in the year 2023 relative to the previous year. Such statistics are produced by CMS each year.

Exhibit 1: 2023 National Health Expenditures FactSheet[a]

- NHE grew 7.5% to $4.9 trillion, or $14,570 per person, and accounted for 17.6% of Gross Domestic Product (GDP)
- Medicare spending grew 8.1% to $1,029.8 billion in 2023, or 21 percent of total NHE.
- Medicaid spending grew 7.9% to $871.7 billion in 2023, or 18 percent of total NHE.
- Private health insurance spending grew 11.5% to $1,464.6 billion in 2023, or 30 percent of total NHE.
- Out of pocket spending grew 7.2% to $505.7 billion in 2023, or 10 percent of total NHE.

[a] Centers for Medicare and Medicaid Services (https://www.cms.gov/Research-Statistics-Data-and-Systems/Statistics-Trends-and-Reports/NationalHealthExpendData/NHE-Fact-Sheet)

1.3 Review

Let us test our understanding so far of the US healthcare system. Consider the following questions.

Q.1 Which of the following numbers comes the closest to the annual average healthcare expenditures per person in the USA (all sources combined)? [Before answering this question, you may want to access US per capita income statistics, which are available from the US Census Bureau website at https://www.census.gov/quickfacts/fact/table/US/SEX255219.]

- $3000
- $6000
- $9000
- $12,000
- $15,000

Q.2 Based on what you have read so far, discuss the pros and cons of each of the following strategies to reduce waste in the US healthcare system. You may use AI tools to help search for examples:

- Change how USG pays for healthcare. Discuss what needs to change.
- Change how providers are paid. Discuss how, and the pros and cons of different approaches.
- Change healthcare operations from within. Discuss how. An example will help.
- Intensify competition among healthcare delivery institutions. Discuss how. An example will help.
- Encourage innovation in the healthcare ecosystem. Discuss how. An example will help.

Q.3 Research and write a couple of paragraphs why health insurance is employer-based insurance for working adults in the USA. Why did this practice evolve? Why did the USG implement the Medicare insurance program only for the elderly?

Answers for Review Questions

Q1. If you answered \$15,000, then you would be correct. In your opinion, is this level of spending good or bad? Should there be attempts to curb such expenditures?

Q2. Student answers will vary. Every strategy has pros and cons. There is no panacea.

Q3. Students can access a variety of sources on the Internet, access books, use AI tools, or listen to podcasts describing the evolution of health insurance in the USA.

Chapter 2
What Makes Healthcare Sector Unique

According to the Bureau of Economic Analysis (BEA) statistics, the US first quarter 2022 seasonally adjusted annual GDP stood at $24,386.7 billion, of which personal consumption expenditures on services amounted to $10,864.2 billion. Clearly, services are a major driver of the US economy. Still, productivity (a ratio of outputs to resources consumed) in some service sectors, notably healthcare, remains low. Some argue that this is in part due to the difficulty of measuring outputs. For example, it would be insufficient to measure the outcome of a surgery in terms of the number of days of hospital stay, and its cost in terms of the cost of hospital stay during the episode of care because patient care needs are heterogeneous and one must also consider differences in clinical outcomes. Therefore, health services researchers have proposed outcome measures such as quality-adjusted life years (QALYs). However, despite these efforts, the measurement of productivity in healthcare remains difficult.

Arrow, a two-time Nobel laureate, in his seminal paper (Arrow, 1963), explains the unique features of the provision of medical care that deviate from the operation of a competitive market, i.e., a market in which the services that would be offered and purchased, and the prices that would be paid for them, would be such that the amounts of services available would equal the amounts that individuals would be willing to purchase at the offered priced. These characteristics are as follows:

1. *Unpredictability of demand.* Unlike demand for food, clothing, transportation, and safety, which can be largely predicted and negative outcomes avoided, the nature of demand for healthcare is unique in the sense that the need arises only when there is an illness (with the exception of preventative services). The nature and extent of illness is difficult to predict, although it will have a significant effect on a household's budget.
2. *Physician behavior.* Physicians (key service providers) do not engage in price competition. In fact, you would be hard pressed to know before receiving medical care the amount that your physician's office will charge your insurance company for treating you. What you pay at the time of the visit (e.g., co-pay

D. Gupta, *Healthcare Analytics*, Springer Texts in Business and Economics,
https://doi.org/10.1007/978-3-032-24835-0_2

or coinsurance) is your share of the amount your insurance will pay, which is not what the physician's office will bill your insurance (see Chap. 3). Physicians' and healthcare facilities' conduct is also highly regulated by a variety of laws and regulations.

3. *Uncertainty of outcome.* When you purchase an airline ticket, you know with a fair degree of certainty that you will reach your intended destination, possibly after some delays. If the airline is unable to transport you from your origin to destination, you will receive a refund and possibly other compensation for the inconvenience. For medical care, this is by and large not true. There is a great deal of uncertainty regarding recovery from disease. Furthermore, you do not pay for a particular outcome. Instead, you pay for the expertise of the doctor. Unfortunately, there is a significant difference between your knowledge of the consequences of any prescribed treatment and that of the doctor. Note that the production methods that lead to an outcome may be unknown in many other situations as well, but there is often a good understanding of the quality of the outcome associated with other services we purchase. The consequence of this uncertainty is the inability of the consumer to know the utility of the prescribed treatment.
4. *Availability of supply.* In the USA and probably around the world, there is not a free market for the supply of medical services. Medical professionals' education is heavily subsidized, and the number of seats available in medical schools is controlled. This creates a supply-demand imbalance that may not be corrected by market forces. Moreover, medical equipment is expensive and requires highly trained professionals to operate, which creates barriers to entry.
5. *Pricing policies.* Physicians often heavily subsidize their services to certain populations based on income and ability to pay. Arrangements where physicians are paid a fixed sum in return for providing all medical services to a cohort of patients are relatively recent. The most common payment mechanism is fee for service (FFS), which promotes overutilization of medical services.

Whereas one or more of the above characteristics may also apply to other industries, e.g., legal and educational services, the combination of all of these in healthcare markets creates a situation in which a competitive equilibrium does not exist. Therefore, government interventions in the form of subsidies and taxes do not bring about the desired social outcomes.

2.1 Review

Q.1 Which of the following is a true and a unique characteristic of health insurance in the USA?

- It is provided to everyone who pays taxes.

- The risk of loss is known.
- The range of outcomes is known.
- The insurance contract is for inputs, not outcomes.
- It is an effective mechanism for risk pooling.

Q.2 Compare and contrast healthcare with educational services. Write down your answers to the following questions first and then compare your answers to those you would obtain for your choice of healthcare services:

- What made you choose the school you are enrolled in?
- How did you estimate the quality of education you might receive prior to joining your school?
- Do you think there exists an imbalance between supply and demand? Would you support a system in which supply shortages resulted in higher prices until the demand would match the supply?
- Do you think your school has a uniform pricing policy, blind to the students' ability to pay?
- Did you have a reasonable expectation of the outcome when you decided to embark on your education? What outcome did you anticipate?

Answers for Review Questions

The review questions require discussion in class. For example, the risk pooling aspect of standard insurance contracts that is common in other situations such as auto and home insurance is difficult to achieve in healthcare. Patients choose insurance contracts based on their expected fixed (insurance premiums) and recurring (such as co-pay, coinsurance, and deductible) costs. Insurance providers engage in complex two-way interactions with providers and patients. These features make it hard to create and price risk pools that are socially optimal.

Q1. The correct answer is "The insurance contract is for inputs, not outcomes."

Q2. Answers will vary. In broad terms, healthcare and educational services have a lot in common. However, there are some crucial differences as well. Some points are mentioned below:

  - Metrics for the quality of education are more readily available and easier to understand.
  - Cost of obtaining education is transparent.
  - Students typically know the tangible outcome in advance, e.g., earning a diploma or certificate.

Chapter 3
Health Insurance Basics

Insurance companies negotiate with service providers to determine the payment for each unit of service provided. Service type and intensity are typically measured by the current procedural terminology (CPT) code. Providers set the retail rates for each CPT code—also referred to as the *charge master*. Insurance companies negotiate lower rates with groups of service providers by offering to list them as in-network providers. Beneficiaries incur a lower cost if they receive services from providers designated as in-network providers, which increases their demand. Depending on the negotiating power of the insurance company and the service providers, the amount of discount over standard fees, often referred to as *provider responsibility*, can be a significant percentage of the charge master fees.

3.1 Insurance Terms

Several terms are commonly used by insurers. These are as follows:

1. *Explanation of Benefits* (EOB): This is a statement that the insurer sends to the beneficiary upon completion of a service episode. It lists standard charges, provider responsibility, and the beneficiary portion of costs.
2. *Co-pay:* For many services, particularly diagnostic services and office visits, the beneficiaries pay a fixed fee that is independent of the amount that the provider receives from the insurance company. This is referred to as the co-pay amount.
3. *Coinsurance:* For some services, e.g., surgical services, insurance plans cover a percentage of the total cost, and the remainder is the responsibility of the beneficiary. The latter is referred to as the coinsurance amount.
4. *Deductible:* Insurance plans specify an amount that the beneficiary must pay out of pocket before any charges will be paid by the insurance company. This is referred to as the deductible amount. It may be different for different types of

D. Gupta, *Healthcare Analytics*, Springer Texts in Business and Economics,
https://doi.org/10.1007/978-3-032-24835-0_3

services, and for individual versus family coverage. Typically, deductible does not apply to preventative services.
5. *Recognized amount:* The difference between the standard charges and the provider responsibility is referred to as the recognized amount. This is the maximum amount that the insurance plan will reimburse for the services provided.

In addition to the above, there is usually an annual maximum that a beneficiary could be asked to pay. This is the combined total of deductible, co-pay, and coinsurance.

3.2 EOB

We begin by examining a hypothetical "explanation of benefits" document shown in Fig. 3.1. Insurance companies post such documents on the web for patient education—see, for example, https://www.bcbstx.com/docs/tx/understanding-eob-tx.pdf. In Fig. 3.1, under the heading "Service Detail," the column labeled "Service Description" lists various services provided. The next three columns show plan calculations, further divided into amounts billed, adjustments, and amounts eligible. The billed amount is the standard charge of the provider (also known as charge master amount). The adjustments, also referred to as *provider responsibility*, are the discounts offered by in-network providers. The difference of these columns is the eligible amount, or *recognized amount*, if the expense category is covered under the plan. If not, then the eligible amount is zero—for example, the health technician charge is not covered for the patient's plan in the sample document. The next three columns are amounts that health plan member is responsible for. These are referred to as member share and comprise deductibles and co-pay, coinsurance, and amounts not covered. In this example, the patient had an outstanding deductible of $1000, and the plan coinsurance rate was 20%. There was a co-pay for diagnostic imaging and medications, but no coinsurance. In the end, the plan paid $1914, the member was responsible for $1766, and the provider received $3680, which was approximately 40% of total charges.

The sample EOB is for in-network providers. The insurers apply similar adjustments to out-of-network providers as well. The difference is that such providers have not committed to charging only the eligible amounts. Therefore, the beneficiary is responsible for all charges that the insurance does not pay. Also, the deductibles and coinsurance rates are typically higher for out-of-network providers. Therefore, the member's share is significantly higher. In this example, if the coinsurance rate and deductible mount were to remain the same, but the provider was an out-of-network provider, then the member would be responsible for $7236, while the plan would still pay $1914. This creates a high financial burden for patients who go out of network and gives insurance companies leverage to negotiate discounts with in-network providers. We consider an example next to highlight the difference between member's responsibility for in-network and out-of-network providers.

Health Plan Claim Summary

MAILING RECIPIENT
Any Beneficiary
245 Sample Lane
Unit ABC
Example City, ST 12345

SUBSCRIBER INFORMATION
Any Company Select Plan

Understanding This Statement

This document explains how a medical claim was evaluated under a health benefit plan. It shows the provider's original charges, any pricing adjustments, the amount considered for benefits, and the member's share of the cost.

This summary is not a bill. A provider may send a separate invoice for any remaining balance.

For questions about this example, contact the plan administrator or customer support team listed on your coverage materials.

Claim overview	
Total provider charges	$9,150.00
Adjustments and prior payments	-$5,470.00
Member responsibility	$1,766.00
Health Plan Responsibility	**$1,914.00**

Member responsibility	
Deductible and cost-sharing	$1,200.00
Coinsurance	$466.00
Amount not covered	$100.00
Estimated amount you may owe	**$1,766.00**

Service detail

Patient: Any Beneficiary **Provider:** Outpatient Center **Claim Ref:** CLM-240404-17
Date of Service: 04/04/2024 **Processed:** 06/20/2024 **Plan Type:** PPO Example

Service description	Plan calculation			Member share		
	Billed	Adjustment	Eligible	Ded./Copay	Coinsurance	Not covered
Room charge	5,000.00	2,800.00	2,200.00	1,000.00	240.00	0.00
Observation / recovery	1200.00	710.00	490.00	0.00	98.00	0.00
Medical supplies	300.00	140.00	160.00	0.00	32.00	0.00
Health Technician	100.00	0.00	0.00	0.00	0.00	100.00
Laboratory tests	1,200.00	820.00	380.00	0.00	76.00	0.00
Additional lab charges	200.00	160.00	40.00	0.00	8.00	0.00
Diagnostic imaging	850.00	690.00	160.00	150.00	0.00	0.00
Medications	200.00	110.00	90.00	50.00	0.00	0.00
Manual therapy	100.00	40.00	60.00	0.00	12.00	0.00
Totals	**9,150.00**	**5,470.00**	**3,580.00**	**1,200.00**	**466.00**	**100.00**

Notes. The eligible amount is the portion considered under the terms of the plan after adjustments are applied. Amounts shown in the member-share columns represent cost participation or charges that do not qualify for plan payment. Member coinsurance rate is 20% for this provider (an in-network provider) The plan pays $3,580 - $1,200 - $466 = $1,914.00. The provider receives $3,680.00.

Fig. 3.1 Sample explanation of benefits

Example 3.1 A patient is treated at a hospital for a minor surgery. The hospital bills $3000 for the service. The insurance company's recognized amount is $1800. The insurance company charges 10% coinsurance for in-network providers and 30% coinsurance for out-of-network providers. The patient has satisfied all deductibles' requirements. This means they have paid an amount equal to their deductible for previous services during the current plan year:

1. How much does the insurance company pay if the provider is in network? How much does the patient pay if the provider is in network?
2. How much does the insurance company pay if the provider is out of network? How much does the patient pay if the provider is out of network?

The Answer If the provider is in network, the insurance company will pay 90% of the recognized amount and the patient will pay 10%. Note that there is no unsatisfied deductible. Therefore, the insurance company pays $1620 and the patient pays $180.

If the provider is out of network, the beneficiary's obligation is not limited to the recognized amount. Moreover, the insurance company will pay only 70% of the recognized amount. Therefore, the insurance company pays $1260 and the patient pays $1740.

Note that the difference can be quite large. This serves as a strong incentive for patients to seek services from in-network providers, and that in turn provides insurance companies the leverage they need to negotiate deep discounts.

3.3 Review

Q.1 Dr. Seuss undergoes a minor surgical procedure on an outpatient basis at an in-network surgery center. A few weeks later, his insurance company sends him an explanation of benefits (EOB), which shows total billed amount of $4200, provider responsibility of $1800, deductible of $500, and a coinsurance rate of 20%. How much will Dr. Seuss have to pay out of pocket after receiving the EOB?

- $880
- $2400
- $980
- $2020
- $1340

Q.2 Physicians are typically paid on a fee-for-service basis for each CPT code. Several alternate payment mechanisms have been proposed and implemented as part of the healthcare reform movement. Research and prepare a list of pros and cons of the following payment mechanisms. Selected students may be asked to lead discussions on each topic:

- Capitation based (per patient)
- Capitation based (population)
- Bundled payments
- Shared savings
- Value based

Answers for Review Questions

Q1. The correct answer is $880. It may be calculated as follows. The recognized amount equals $4200 − $1800 = $2400. Because Dr. Seuss has $500 deductible, the insurance company will be responsible for $2400 − $500 =

\$1900. Dr. Seuss's share of the recognized amount will be (0.2)(1900) = \$380. He will therefore pay \$380 + \$500 = \$880 in total.

Some students may provide the answer that Dr. Seuss will need to pay \$980. That answer is obtained by first calculating Dr. Seuss's share as (0.2)(2400) = \$480 and then adding the \$500 deductible to that amount. That approach has Dr. Seuss paying the deductible and an additional 20% on the deductible, making his effective deductible as \$600. Therefore, that is not the correct answer.

Q2. Answers will vary. Instructors are encouraged to use a class session to discuss pros and cons of such approaches. An example is presented next.

Students may use AI tools to help with background research. This requires students to engineer precise prompts. An example prompt is provided below.

```
You are helping an advanced undergraduate student to write an essay
    on per patient capitation payment regime for healthcare
    services. It is sometimes called HMO (Health Maintenance
    Organization) approach. Provide a precise and succinct summary
    of the concept and its pros and cons. List all sources of
    information you used.
```

Chapter 4
Capacity Calculations

Managing healthcare operations involves matching supply with demand in a high-stakes environment with little room for mistakes. Managers are often tasked with calculating the capacity of a particular configuration and provision of resources. In general, this is a difficult task. However, it is not difficult to calculate a *theoretical maximum capacity* as we will find out in this chapter. In fact, there are four interrelated concepts that will be discussed in this chapter. These are as follows:

1. *Bottleneck Resource:* The resource with the smallest maximum rate.
2. *Theoretical maximum capacity:* The production rate of the bottleneck resource.
3. *Utilization:* Long-term fraction of time that a resource is busy.
4. *Throughput Rate:* The rate at which patients are served by the clinic. It is the smaller of the production rate of the bottleneck resource and the demand rate.

As the name suggests, the bottleneck in a production process (in this case the production of healthcare services) is the rate-limiting resource, i.e., the capacity of this resource will limit the rate at which we would be able to produce services if demand were unlimited. We can identify a bottleneck without knowledge of demand rate. However, to calculate the utilization and the throughput rate, we need to know the demand rate. Therefore, we shall first calculate the theoretical maximum capacity and identify the bottleneck resource without specifying the demand rate in an example. After that, we shall calculate the utilization and the throughput rate for given values of the demand rate.

Example 4.1 The context is a primary[1] care clinic. The typical patient flow (i.e., how patients experience service) is shown in Fig. 4.1.

The clinic has two medical assistants (MAs), one nurse, one MD, and five exam rooms. Figure 4.1 uses triangles to represent patient waiting and rectangles to denote

[1] Primary care typically includes family medicine, internal medicine, pediatrics, and obstetrics and gynecology.

D. Gupta, *Healthcare Analytics*, Springer Texts in Business and Economics,
https://doi.org/10.1007/978-3-032-24835-0_4

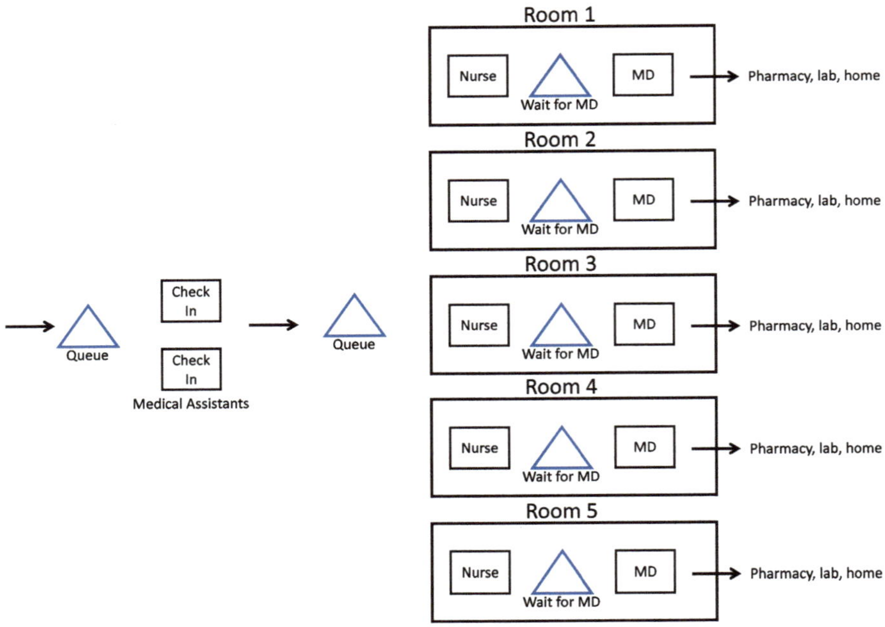

Fig. 4.1 Patient flow diagram

various resources—MAs, nurse, MD and the exam rooms. It is a good practice to also show the service time of each resource on the same diagram. See if you can do so. Suppose we only have limited data about mean service times—shown below.

Resource	Number	Mean service time (mins)	Unit rate (/hour)
Medical assistants (MAs)	2	10	6
Nurses (RNs)	1	10	6
Exam rooms	5	40	1.5
MDs	1	30	2

Note that unit rate = average number of patients served per hour per resource. Using this definition, the unit rate of MAs is $\frac{60}{10} = 6$ patients per hour. Other values of the unit rate column are calculated in a similar fashion.

Given this data, can we calculate the maximum number of patients this clinic can handle per hour? Are the data provided sufficient? Do we need additional data such as the standard deviation of service times? Do we need to know service protocols, e.g., which patients have priority?

The Answer We can calculate the theoretical maximum capacity but not the realized throughput and utilization without additional information. The provided data are sufficient only for that purpose. We do not need to know the variability of service times or the service protocol. We obtain the solution as follows.

The theoretical maximum capacity is 2 patients/hour, or 15 patients during a 7.5 hour day, and MD is the bottleneck resource. How did we arrive at this conclusion? We arrived at these conclusions by performing the following calculations.

Resource	Number	Service time (mins)	Unit rate	Max rate
Medical assistants	2	10	6	12
Nurses	1	10	6	6
Exam rooms	5	40	1.5	7.5
MDs	1	30	2	2

Note that Max Rate = (Unit Rate)∗(the number of resources). The Max Rate is the maximum number of patients that a particular resource can serve in an hour if it never idled, i.e., if there were always a sufficient number of patients waiting for this resource. That is, Max Rate = (Unit Rate)∗(Number of copies of the resource). The theoretical maximum capacity is the smallest of the Max Rate across all resources.

Utilization of each resource is the minimum of 1 and the ratio of the demand rate to the Max rate. Note that utilization cannot exceed 1 because when that happens the patients' waiting time will become unstable with demand exceeding at least one resource's capacity to handle patients. Utilization of each resource is calculated in the table below upon assuming a demand rate of two patients per hour, which is the maximum demand rate that the clinic can handle. We note that the MD has the maximum utilization and that at a demand rate of two patients per hour, the MD is fully utilized and the throughput rate of the clinic is as high as it can be.

Resource	Number	Service time	Max rate	Utilization
Medical assistants	2	10	12	$= 2/12 = 0.167$
Nurses	1	10	6	$= 2/6 = 0.333$
Exam rooms	5	40	7.5	$= 2/7.5 = 0.267$
MDs	1	30	2	$= 2/2 = 1$

The throughput rate[2] is the minimum of the bottleneck rate and the demand rate. One may think of throughput rate as the rate at which patients are leaving the clinic after being served. Note that we did not need to know the probability distribution of service times or which patients have priority in order to identify the bottleneck resource and calculate the theoretical maximum capacity, utilization, and throughput rate. Of course, these calculations pertain to what is theoretically achievable. In practice, there are a whole host of factors that will limit a clinic's ability to realize the theoretical maximums.

Let us next consider a slightly more involved example. Additional practice problems can be found in Sect. 5.3.

[2] In a system with no patient attrition Throughput Rate = min{Bottleneck rate, Demand rate}.

Example 4.2 An integrated practice unit (IPU) has two medical assistants (MAs), two nurse practitioner (NP), one MD (half time), one social worker (SW), and one physical therapist (PT). All patients first register with MAs, complete some forms, and then wait for their turn to be taken to an exam room. Registration takes 15 minutes on average. There are six exam rooms. Patients are first seen by an NP who determines whether the patient is a complex case or not. Complex cases, about 25% of all patients, are referred to the MD. The patient does not leave the exam room, but waits for the MD. Complex patients are typically not seen by any other service provider. NP average consult times for the complex patients are 25 minutes and MD average consult times are 30 minutes.

If the NP labels a patient as not complex, then he or she may see a combination of SW and PT. Patients remain in the exam room, and the service providers visit them to provide consultation. Approximately, 20% of the noncomplex patients need to be seen only by the SW, 50% by PT only, and 30% by both SW and PT. The average consult times are 30 minutes with the SW and 20 minutes with the PT. The sequence of consultation with the SW and the PT does not matter. The NP spends on average 15 minutes with noncomplex patients. What is the theoretical maximum capacity of this clinic? A brief description of IPUs is provided in Exhibit 2.

Exhibit 2: The Integrated Practice Unit

Example 2 is motivated by a relatively new concept in the delivery of healthcare adopted by the Dell Medical School at UT Austin. Under this paradigm, patients are provided complete care for closely related groups of diagnoses in each visit. This avoids the need to consult multiple experts for certain diagnoses,e.g. patients with back pain may need to consult with nurses, MDs, social workers, physical therapists, and psychiatrists [Jay+19]. The patient remains in the same exam room. Different providers visit the patient as needed. There is some flexibility in the sequence in which different providers may provide consultation. A key challenge for managers of such clinics is operational efficiency and calculation of IPU capacity. The example presented in this book greatly simplifies the real capacity calculation problem.

The Answer The answer hinges upon understanding that there are two primary patient types—complex (25%) and noncomplex (75%). Noncomplex patients are further divided into three types—those who need to be seen only by the SW (20%), those who need to be seen only by the PT (50%), and those who need to be seen by both the SW and the PT (30%). Although the NP sorts the patients into these categories, they do not make a patient complex or noncomplex, nor do they determine the patients' needs in terms of who they need to see. The needs of patients depend on the medical/clinical symptoms they present. The NP may not be perfect and may make a mistake in sorting patients. For now, we shall not consider errors in sorting patients. Let us next write the resource time requirements by patient type.

Type	Percent	MA	NP	MD	SW	PT	Room
Complex	25%	15	25	30	0	0	55
Not complex – SW	15%	15	15	0	30	0	45
Not complex – PT	37.5%	15	15	0	0	20	35
Not complex – SW + PT	22.5%	15	15	0	30	20	65
Average		15	17.5	7.5	11.25	12	48.25

To obtain the averages, we multiply the resource use times with the percentages as demonstrated for the NP below.

$$\text{NP Average} = 25 * 0.25 + 15 * 0.75 = 17.5.$$

Students may be asked to draw a patient flow diagram to represent the IPU. A possible patient flow diagram is shown in Sect. 4.3.

We are now ready to perform calculations similar to those we did for the previous example. We obtain the following table upon assuming a demand rate of four patients per hour.

Resource	Number	Service time	Unit rate	Max rate	Utilization
MAs	2	15	4	8	0.50
NPs	2	17.5	3.43	6.86	0.58
MDs	0.5	7.5	8	4	1.00
SW	1	11.25	5.33	5.33	0.75
PT	1	12	5	5	0.80
Exam rooms	6	48.25	1.24	7.46	0.54

We observe that Unit rate = 60/Service Time = hourly rate per resource, Max Rate = (Unit Rate)*(Number of Resources), MD is the bottleneck resource, and that the theoretical maximum capacity is four patients per hour.

Is 100% utilization reachable? Is it a reasonable target? What may go wrong? The answers are that 100% utilization is often nor achievable, that in most cases, it is not a reasonable target, and that the primary reason for the discrepancy is variability. Let us look deeper into these issues next.

Why 100% Utilization Is Not Achievable? One hundred percent utilization is not a realizable target because a whole host of reasons can cause the actual capacity to be significantly less than the theoretical maximum capacity. This happens when the bottleneck resource idles because of variability in demand for physician services and patient preferences, or the service processes, or both:

- Variability (caused by time-of-day, day-of-week, and seasonal patterns, as well as patient and provider heterogeneity):
  - Number and type of appointment requests
  - Provider availability
  - Service times
  - No-shows and cancelations

- Patient preferences:
  - Day and time of appointment
  - PCP (preferred or primary care provider) match

These factors typically result in patient waiting and cause queues to form. Clinics respond by carefully scheduling patient arrivals and sequencing services in a manner that avoids idling. Still, some idling cannot be avoided, resulting in resource capacity being wasted. For instance, in the IPU example, there may be patients needing the services of a PT, the PT may be free, but not able to serve those patients because they are either waiting for or being served by another service provider. Careful sequencing and scheduling of patients could serve to minimize such events.

All of the reasons mentioned above relate to variability of some sort. If all patients and providers were identical, their arrival patterns and service times deterministic, it would be possible to minimize (though perhaps not eliminate) wasting resource capacity. Please look at a thought experiment described on the next page for developing greater intuition about variability. That begs the question whether variability is always bad. The answer is not always. *Synchronized variability* can be beneficial. It is the type of variability that is deliberately introduced in response to an exogenous variability. For example, when a physician adjusts available number of slots (introduces supply variability) in response to realized demand for appointments. When exogenous variability is unavoidable, a small amount of synchronized variability typically improves performance significantly. *How? Can you demonstrate the value of synchronized variability through an example?*

Exhibit 3: Why Variability Matters

Consider two walk-in clinics (labeled A and B) with a single MD, identical average number of arrivals each day, and the same average service time for each patient. Suppose the clinics are open for 8 hours each day from 8 AM through 4 PM. The average daily arrival rate is 4 patients per hour and the average service rate is 5 patients per hour. This implies the average inter-arrival time is 15 minutes and the average service time is 12 minutes. Upon examining data from these clinics, suppose you find that clinic A has much longer average patient wait times than clinic B. What could explain this difference?

We construct a thought experiment to explain the role of variability. Suppose at clinic B, patients arrive at 8:00 AM, 8:15 AM, 8:30 AM, $\cdots$, 3:45 PM, i.e., inter-arrival times are not variable. Let us also assume that the MD at clinic B takes exactly 12 minutes to serve each patient. Then, no patient who arrives at clinic B will experience wait time! The average wait time will be zero.

Suppose clinic A's MD can also serve each patient in exactly 12 minutes. However, the patient arrivals are not equally spaced. In particular, suppose 16 patients arrive at 8 AM, and the remaining 16 arrive at noon. Then, only the first and the 17th patients will not wait. All others will experience some waiting. This is a simple example that illustrates the impact of variability. In reality, both inter-arrival and service times are variable, and furthermore random.

4.1 Patient Appointments

The ability to respond to variability (e.g., by flexing capacity) is often limited. How do then healthcare providers cope with variability? A common remedy is the use of appointment systems.[3] Appointments help to:

- Smooth flow.
- Maximize service providers' efficiency.
- Allow service providers to manage their daily workload.

Appointments for medical services lower patients' in-clinic wait times, particularly its variance. There are two types of waiting time:

- Direct (in clinic)
- Indirect (to access an appointment)

Many patients prefer to wait in the comfort of their home and show up only when the provider is available to see them. Waiting at home is an example of indirect wait time. It is much less costly for patients. The magnitudes of these two types of waiting times are also different. Direct wait times are measured in minutes, whereas indirect waiting times are often measured in days, or even weeks and months. In practice, clinics need to balance different types of waiting times because patients have different preferences for different types of waiting, depending on the urgency and a whole host of other factors. For this reason, many clinics offer a mix of walk-in access and appointments-only access to providers. Others offer urgent or after-hour clinics for walk-in patients who cannot wait for an appointment. We will discuss the challenges that operations managers face when thinking about the design of appointment systems in Chap. 7.

4.2 Relationship Between Average Backlog and Average Waiting Time

Many health systems can be thought of as queueing systems (see Appendix A.2), with patients being the customers and resources such as MDs being the servers. Each such system can be described in terms of the following parameters:

1. Average patient arrival rate
2. Average patient service time
3. Average backlog of patients waiting to be served

[3] There are many publications dealing with the design of appointment systems, e.g., (Gupta & Wang, 2012). Interested students are encouraged to seek such resources from the library.

A system is said to be *stable* if the backlog possesses a *steady-state* distribution, i.e., the backlog does not consistently build up over time. A minimum requirement for a system to be stable is that the average service rate must exceed the average arrival rate of patients. That is, in the long run, the system should be able to provide service at a rate faster than the rate at which service requests arrive. If this were not true, then some patients would not be served, and unless there was attrition (which is sometimes referred to as balking and reneging), the system backlog would continue to build.

In a stable system with no balking or reneging, the average rate at which patients leave after being served (note this is not the same as average service rate) is equal to the average arrival rate. Also, the following equation holds for every stable system with no balking.

$$\text{average backlog} = (\text{average arrival rate}) * (\text{average time in system}). \tag{4.1}$$

The above relationship is also known as the *Little's Law*, named after the scientist who first proved it Little (1961).

4.3 Review

Q.1 Draw a patient flow diagram to represent the IPU.

Q.2 Which other services use appointments? What may be some benefits of using appointments in addition to those mentioned in Sect. 4.1?

Q.3 List some management challenges for appointments only, walk-in only, and hybrid mode of provider access in outpatient clinics.

Answers for Review Questions

Exercise 4.1 Try to show service times on both diagrams (Figs. 4.2 and 4.3).

Exercise 4.2 Legal services, car repair services, recording services (for property deeds, marriage, and births and deaths), and court services are some examples of nonmedical services that allow consumers to make appointments in advance. In addition to the benefits of appointments mentioned in Sect. 4.1, well-designed appointment systems can increase continuity of service, client engagement, server productivity, and revenue.

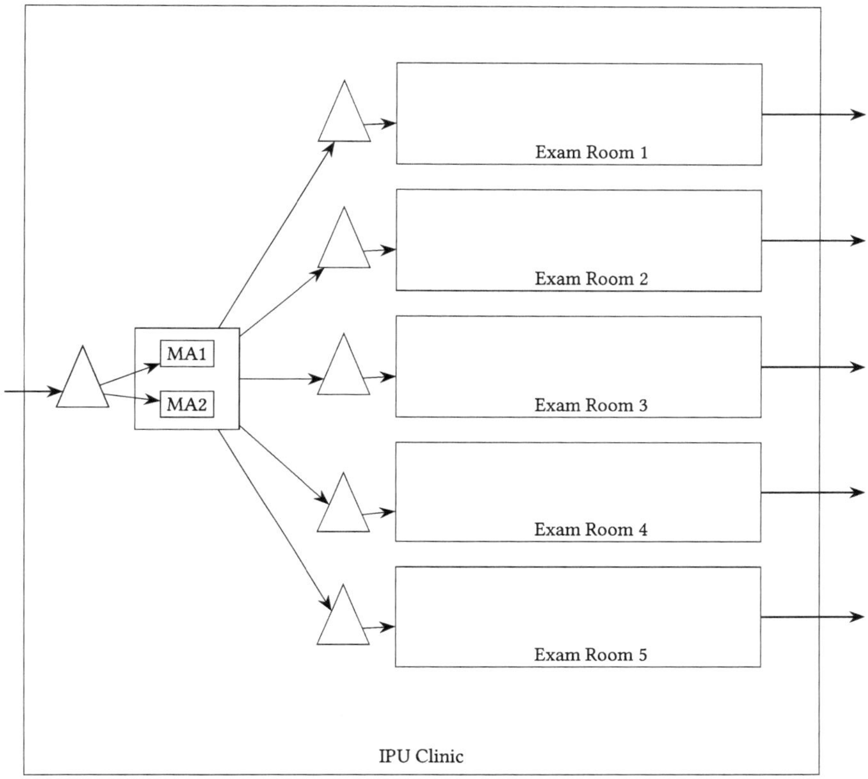

Fig. 4.2 IPU patient flow diagram 1. In this depiction, patients are divided into types by the Triage Nurse in the exam room. Patient interactions with providers within the exam room are shown in Fig. 4.3

Exercise 4.3 Clinics that have no ability to serve walk-in patients lose out on demand from such patients, and patients lose continuity of care. Walk-in clinics need a set of rules to deal with time-varying arrival patterns, e.g., turning away some patients when in-clinic waiting line exceeds a certain limit. Walk-in-only clinics typically offer services for a limited number of diagnoses, e.g., retail clinics like Minute Clinic. They may offer a limited number of appointments during non-busy times. Hybrid clinics can serve demand from patients who need on-demand care, but they need careful management of patient expectations—i.e., how long they may have to wait until health professionals can see them.

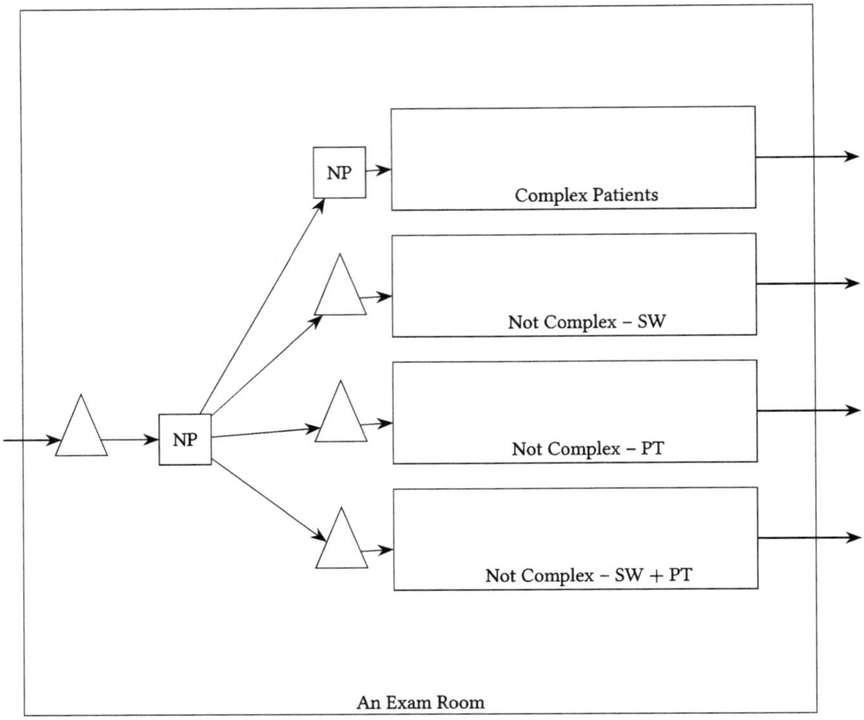

Fig. 4.3 Patients interactions with resources within an exam room. Patients types are identified by the NP. NP time is therefore split into two parts, based on patient complexity—every patient type needs 15 minutes of NP time. Complex patients need an additional 10 minutes. The requirements for other resources are appropriately adjusted for each patient type. Students need to complete the diagram and show resource usage at each stage

Chapter 5
Exercises for Part I

5.1 Discussion Questions

1. What makes healthcare operations different from retail, restaurant, hotel, airline, professional services, . . ., operations?
2. Give an example of a consumer-facing digital front door used by a healthcare provider.
3. Give an example of a back-office operation that could/should be digitized.
4. Should doctors be asked to first consult an AI-driven consultation system before prescribing treatment to patients?

5.2 Multiple-Choice Questions

1. What is a bottleneck resource? Check the single best answer:
   - A resource with the smallest service rate
   - The first resource that patients encounter
   - The most expensive resource
   - A resource that has the largest service rate
   - None of the above
2. Upon collecting appointment call volume data, a clinic finds that on average 15 patients call every day and make an appointment. There are no no-shows and cancelations, the theoretical maximum capacity is 16 patients per day, and the average daily backlog is 30 patients. What is the average wait time experienced by patients? Check the single best answer:
   - Less than 1 day
   - 1.875 days

D. Gupta, *Healthcare Analytics*, Springer Texts in Business and Economics,
https://doi.org/10.1007/978-3-032-24835-0_5

- More than 7 days
- 2 days
- 0.5 days

3. A clinic manager has been asked to prepare a list of factors that contribute to high patient backlog. Which of the following factors should be on her list? Check all factors that apply:
   - The theoretical maximum capacity
   - The arrival process variability
   - Patient no-shows and late cancelations
   - The availability of on-site pharmacy
   - The number of exam rooms
4. Which of the following statements is true?
   - Max rate is always greater than the unit rate.
   - Max rate cannot exceed 1.
   - At a minimum, the number of resources available must be 1.
   - A bottleneck resource has the highest max rate.
   - A bottleneck resource has the highest utilization.
5. Which of the following are often cited as reasons why healthcare is different from the vast majority of other services? Check all that apply:
   - Opaque pricing
   - Informational asymmetry
   - Drug shortages
   - High labor costs
   - Significant government regulation and oversight

5.3 Long-Answer Questions

Problem 5.1 All patients entering a clinic register with the medical assistant (MA), and then wait before being taken to an exam room. Registration takes 10 minutes on average. There are five exam rooms. Patients are seen by a nurse practitioner (NP), who determines whether the patient needs to see only the MD, only the physical therapist (PT), or a PT and social worker (SW). 20% of patients need to see the MD only, 55% need to see the PT only, and the remaining see both the PT and the SW. The NP average consult time is 20 minutes for all patients. The MD on average spends 25 minutes with the patients, the SW spends 20 minutes with the patients, and the PT spends on average 15 minutes with the patients. The clinic has three MAs, two NPs, one MD, two PTs, and one SW:

1. Draw a process flow diagram.
2. Calculate the maximum rate and utilization for each resource.

3. Identify the bottleneck resource and the theoretical maximum capacity of the clinic.

Problem 5.2 A clinic has a theoretical maximum capacity of 16 patients per day. The average backlog is 20 patients, and on average, patients wait four days to enter the clinic. There are no no-shows and cancelations. What is the average arrival rate of patients at this clinic?

Problem 5.3 A patient is treated at an in-network hospital for a minor surgery. The hospital bills \$4000 for the service. The insurance company's recognized amount is \$2200. The insurance company charges 30% coinsurance for in-network providers. The patient has \$500 deductible left for the current plan year:

1. How much will the insurance company pay, and how much will the patient pay?
2. Redo the answer to the above question when the provider is out-of-network provider. In that case, the deductible amount is \$800, and the coinsurance rate is 40%.

Part II
The Outpatient Clinic

Chapter 6
Introduction

If you ask around, you would be hard pressed to find an adult person in the USA who has not experienced the process of booking an appointment to see a doctor. In fact, most people would have clear recollection of having to wait for their appointment, and having to wait for the doctor on the day of their appointment even when they arrived on time. Whereas some waiting is unavoidable because patients' needs are not entirely predictable, a well-designed appointment system aims to achieve simultaneously low patient wait times and high utilization of providers' time. It should also ensure that patients can consult their preferred care providers when they attempt to book appointments. In this part of the book, we will examine the economics of outpatient clinics and strategies clinic managers can use to achieve superior outcomes. But first, let us review some concepts from Part I that are relevant for this discussion, and introduce a few new concepts.

6.1 Key Concepts

The following concepts were introduced in Part I of this book:

- *Bottleneck Resource:* The resource with the smallest maximum rate.
- *Theoretical Maximum Capacity:* The production rate of the bottleneck resource.
- *Utilization:* Long-term fraction of time that a resource is busy.
- *Throughput Rate:* The smaller of the production rate of the bottleneck resource and the demand rate.
- *Synchronized Variability*: When a manager adds variability in response to an exogenous variability, for example, adding extra appointment slots in those instances when advance demand for appointments exceeds the supply.
- *Direct Waiting Time*: In clinic waiting time.
- *Indirect Waiting Time*: Delay in access to an appointment.

D. Gupta, *Healthcare Analytics*, Springer Texts in Business and Economics,
https://doi.org/10.1007/978-3-032-24835-0_6

The following concepts are introduced for the first time in this part of the book:

- *PCP:* Any primary care provider (MD or NP). In some instances, a PCP is a provider who has been selected by at least one patient as their preferred primary care provider.[1]
- *Panel Size*: Count of patients who have either declared or routinely see a particular provider (PCP) for their primary care needs.
- *PCP Match rate*: For each PCP (MD or NP), the percentage of patients belonging to their panel who are seen by that PCP.
- *Spoilage Rate*: The percentage of appointments that are either no-shows or late cancelations.
- *Same-Day Appointments*: Appointments that are booked within 24 hours of the time when the patient calls to book an appointment.
- *PCP Coverage rate*: Percentage of same-day appointment patients seen by a service provider who are not in their panel.

Let us work out a simple example next to learn how to calculate the PCP match rate and the PCP coverage rate. Calculation of the remaining quantities is straightforward. Suppose in a selected time period (say a quarter), a particular provider had 1000 appointments. Let us refer to this provider as Dr. D. During the same time period, patients belonging to Dr. D's panel booked 1200 appointments. Among the 1000 appointments that Dr. D had, suppose 900 were with her panel patients, i.e., with patients who belonged to Dr. D's panel. Then,

$$\text{PCP Match Rate for Dr. D} = \frac{900}{1200} = 0.75. \tag{6.1}$$

PCP match rate is usually expressed as a percentage. So, Dr. D's PCP match rate would be 75%. This also means that 300 patients belonging to Dr. D's panel ended up seeing a different provider for their medical needs. Those patients therefore suffered loss of continuity of care.

Next, suppose that of the 1000 appointments, Dr. D had 100 same-day appointments during the same time period. Among the 100 same-day appointments, suppose 60 were patients who did not belong to Dr. D's panel. Then,

$$\text{PCP Coverage Rate for Dr. D} = \frac{60}{100} = 0.6. \tag{6.2}$$

PCP coverage rate is also expressed as a percentage. So, Dr. D's coverage rate would be 60%. PCP coverage rate is a measure of a doctor's contribution to meeting a clinic's goal of provider faster service to those patients who consider their needs to be urgent.

[1] Often PCP refers to any primary care doctor. In some cases, patients are asked to choose a particular provider in a mutli-provider clinic as their preferred provider for the majority of their routine medical care. Such providers are also called PCPs. This can be confusing.

PCP match rate and PCP coverage rate can be calculated relatively easily from historical data. They provide a quick way to assess both the continuity of care and the degree to which doctors are willing to provide same-day service to meet clinic's goals.

6.2 Payment Paradigms

Historically, medical professionals such as MDs and NPs have been paid on a FFS basis[2] This transfers the financial risk associated with care costs to payers and patients. It also encourages volume over medical necessity and clinical outcomes. Increasingly, payers are attempting to link payments to outcomes. Such an approach is sometimes referred to as *value-based payment* (VBP). In a VBP approach, providers negotiate a budget for specified care needs of a population of patients (relying on the FFS chassis for each service) and a quality-based incentive (top-up payment) that depends on achieving certain clinical outcomes specified by the payer in addition to remaining within budget. The negotiations involve insurers and either groups of providers or health systems. The provider group or the health system bills the payer on an FFS basis and expenditures are tallied annually. Many such schemes provide an upside payment if the provider group remains within budget and meets specified quality standards, but there is no penalty for coming over budget, i.e., there is no downside risk. Some VBP schemes pay provider groups a fixed recurring payment (e.g., per member per month) for providing medical care to a population of patients regardless of the incurred costs. The provider groups usually continue to pay health professionals that belong to the same health system on an FFS basis. They are also responsible for billed services that patients receive from out-of-network providers (i.e., providers outside the health system), which is referred to as "leakage." In such cases, the provider groups also face a downside risk in the sense that they are responsible for costs exceeding their budget. Note that they continue to have the upside potential if they come within budget and meet quality standards. Finally, some contracts provide additional top-up payments for achieving high quality, which are referred to as quality-based payments.

There is significant debate over how one should measure healthcare quality and how quality measures ought to be linked with costs/incentives. Detailed consideration of such issues is beyond the scope of this book. A good starting point

[2] In outpatient (clinic) settings, standard fees are determined for each Current Procedural Terminology (CPT) code. The FFS is the negotiated value of this fee based on negotiations between insurers and providers, which often depends on their respective bargaining powers in each healthcare market. Over time FFS payments only approximately reflect the cost of providing each service. In the inpatient (hospital) setting, fees are largely based on patient discharge codes that have been grouped into *diagnosis related groups* (DRGs). Many insurers pay a fixed fee for a particular DRG, adjusted for patient acuity and market factors, but independent of the actual costs incurred by the hospital for treating each patient. More details will be provided later.

for students in this topic is the website maintained by the National Quality Forum https://www.qualityforum.org/Home.aspx from which one can access numerous reports on the topic. Also, students interested in the topic of healthcare quality will find it useful to read (Committee on Quality of Health Care in America and Institute of Medicine, 2001).

6.3 The Economics of Outpatient Clinics

Ambulatory or outpatient care services comprise the bulk of patients' encounters with healthcare professionals. The vast majority of office visits are planned, i.e., patients contact the physicians' offices in advance to book an appointment. The following statistics tell this story:

- 1 B = physician office visits (2019–2024, source: https://www.cdc.gov/nchs/data/ahcd/namcs_summary/2019-namcs-web-tables-508.pdf)
- 50.3% = primary care appointments
- 29% = other medical specialties appointments
- 20.7% = surgical specialists appointments
- Most office-based services are organized around medium to large group practices

We shall focus on primary care services because they are the bulk of services provided on an outpatient basis. 85.2% of adults in 2024 reported visiting a doctor of other health care provider (Source: https://www.cdc.gov/nchs/fastats/physician-visits.htm#print).

What are some common organization structures you have encountered when visiting primary care clinics? How should a clinic manager think about organizing clinic operations? While most of us are familiar with medium to large group practices, the next two examples are less common. However, such patterns of practice are on the rise.

Exhibit 4: Solo Practice

In a Family Practice Medicine article (2007, 14(6):19–24), Dr. Brian Forrest wrote "Seven years ago, I began exploring ways I could practice medicine without the hassles and pressures of managed care. I also wanted to find a way to reduce fees significantly for uninsured and underinsured patients. For more than a year, I read about practice innovations and observed other practices. I used what I learned to develop a model that, so far at least, seems to achieve my goals. Here's how it works:

- We charge our patients a flat rate for office visits. Currently, the fee is $45.
- We do not file insurance; our patients pay at the time of their visit.
- We do not sign contracts with insurance companies."

Do you think Dr. Forrest is likely to succeed going forward? What challenges would he have faced?

Exhibit 5: Concierge Medicine

For a flat monthly fee, concierge medicine offers the advantage of quick access to primary care providers via office or virtual visits with no co-pays, deductibles or co-insurance. The doctor may provide a bill that patients may use to get reimbursement from their health insurance, usually as an out-of-network provider. The doctor coordinates specialist referrals and/or hospital care as needed, but the patient needs regular insurance coverage for those. Patients pay a one-time initiation fee and monthly charges, which can vary from a few thousand to tens of thousands of dollars a year. See https://www.forbes.com/health/healthy-aging/concierge-medicine/#footnote_2 for additional information about concierge medicine.

Do you think concierge medicine is the remedy for long wait times and confusing billing practices in health care delivery?

These examples suggest that a useful way to categorize organizational structures is either by provider count, or patient volume, or both. There is one more relevant dimension that we call the mode of delivery. Along those lines, emerging modes of delivery are *Retail clinics*, *Telemedicine*-only clinics, and *hybrid* (in-person + telemedicine) clinics. We shall not discuss them in detail in this book. These structures provide new challenges for operations managers. For example, retail clinics provide quick, convenient, low-cost, and on-demand service for relatively few clinical diagnoses. Many such clinics are colocated with pharmacies. In order to succeed, such clinics need to standardize service protocols, keep costs low, and serve a large volume of patients.

Telemedicine clinics depend on seamless technology, convenience, and short wait times to attract patients. They often work well for clinical conditions that do not require physical contact between the patients and the provider. Hybrid clinics face the additional complexity of interleaving in-person and virtual appointments, which significantly complicates the design of appointment systems.

6.3.1 Models for Organizing Clinics

When choosing a clinic's organizational structure, a manager must first think about the customer-service model, i.e., how the clinic will attract and retain patients, and then harmonize the revenue and operational models to work in concert with the customer-service model. From there, we arrive at the following three key concepts.

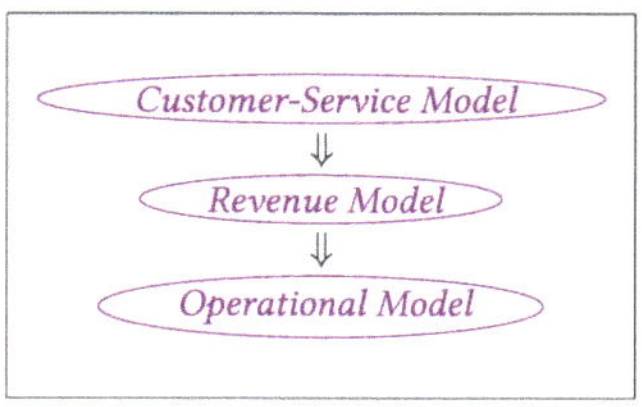

The customer-service model can be classified into three groups based on volume: high-volume, low-volume, and solo practices. The choice of the model will depend on provider's preferences, the market in which the clinic operates, its competition, and needs of the families. For example, while many solo practitioners choose that practice style because of their convictions about how best to serve patients, different families may prefer different customer-service models and it may be difficult to satisfy different types of family needs via a single model. We next discuss the implications of each customer-service model on the appropriate choice of corresponding revenue and operational models:

- High-volume group practice $\longleftrightarrow$ insurance + range of services.
- Low-volume concierge medicine $\longleftrightarrow$ annual retainer + range of services.
- Low-volume solo $\longleftrightarrow$ cash-only + stripped-down services.

High-volume clinics need to accept most forms of insurance in order to survive. Clinic managers need to:

- Focus on optimizing the use of bottleneck resource time (usually the MD).
- Sustain high support staff costs $\Rightarrow$ large panels. The concept of panels is discussed in Sect. 7.1.
- Carefully orchestrate roles, schedules, and protocols $\Rightarrow$ standardization.

Low-volume concierge practice requires an adequate number of patients willing to pay annual retainers or monthly fees. Clinic managers must:

- Focus on patient experience $\Rightarrow$ customization.
- Ensure direct and quick access to MD $\Rightarrow$ relatively small panels.
- Operate in a region with sufficient affluent population.

Solo practices are often low-cost alternatives to those who have no insurance or inadequate insurance. Clinic managers (often the solo providers themselves) need to:

- Focus on cutting costs $\Rightarrow$ no staff.
- Direct access $\Rightarrow$ remove gatekeepers.
- Aim to serve uninsured or underinsured population.

6.3.2 Revenue and Cost Calculations

How many patients does an MD need to see every day under the three different models if he or she wants to earn \$100K annual pay? In this section, we work out three hypothetical examples to highlight the differences among the three organizational structures. To begin, we need to understand the different types of costs and revenues that we need to consider. We also need to make certain assumptions about numerical values of costs and revenues for the purpose of developing illustrative examples. A list follows.

Revenues

- Daily revenue = Patients per day∗realized revenue per patient (note that realized revenue is often less than the charged amount—see Chap. 3).

Expenditures

- Fixed costs—MA salary, malpractice insurance, utilities, certain medical supplies, rent
- Variable costs—outsourced lab tests, consumables such as syringes

Assumptions

- Solo practitioner charges \$45 for office visit and \$37 for lab charges and supplies for a total charge of \$82 per visit.
- Concierge and group practice MDs bill for each visit. Realized revenue \$110 per visit. Group practice directly bills the insurance, whereas concierge practice provides the bill to the patient who must claim reimbursement from their insurance. The patient pays the entire bill up front.[3]
- Concierge service provider also charges an additional \$500 per patient per year enrollment fee.
- There are 245 working days in a year, and each patient makes on average three appointments per year.
- Salary and fixed costs of the practice:
  - Solo practitioner: \$20,000
  - Concierge: 162,000
  - Group practice: \$142,000
- Variable costs: 20% of revenue—same for all three models.

Sample Calculations

x = number of appointments per day
n = number of enrolled patients (relevant only for concierge model)

Solo

$$x = \frac{100{,}000 + 20{,}000}{0.8 * 82 * 245} = 7.46 \longrightarrow 8 \text{ per day.}$$

The numerator in the above expression is the total annual revenue that the solo practitioner needs to generate, and the denominator is the effective revenue if the practitioner had one appointment per day during the year. Because a patient makes three appointments in a year, in order to generate $8 * 245$ appointments in the year, the solo practitioner clinic needs to have $8 * 245/3 = 653.3 \approx 654$ registered patients.

[3] When patients pay minimum monthly charges, visit expenses are offset against the monthly fees.

Group Practice

$$x = \frac{100{,}000 + 142{,}000}{0.8 * 110 * 245} = 11.2 \longrightarrow 12 \text{ per day}.$$

The numerator in the above expression is the total annual revenue that the practitioner in a group practice needs to generate and the denominator is the effective revenue if the practitioner had one appointment per day during the year. Because a patient makes three appointments in a year, in order to generate $12 * 245$ appointments in the year, the solo practitioner clinic needs to have $12*245/3 = 980$ registered patients.

Concierge

$$n = \frac{100{,}000 + 162{,}000}{500 + 0.8 * 110 * 3} = 342.93$$

$$x = \frac{n \times 3}{245} = 4.2 \longrightarrow 5 \text{ per day}.$$

In the first equation, we calculate the number of patients who must register with the practice to generate the revenue needed to sustain the practice and the practitioner's pay. The numerator is the total amount needed. The denominator is the revenue per enrollee, which equals the \$500 retainer and the effective annual revenue per enrollee assuming three appointments per year. That is, the concierge practitioner needs to enroll 343 patients willing to pay the retainer. The second equation calculates the number of daily appointments that will be necessary to serve 343 enrolled patients.

While the above calculations depend on the various assumptions we made, the qualitative insights from these calculations are generally true. Note that the annual number of patients needed by each type of practitioner may be viewed as the required panel size in each practice model. To summarize, we find that:

- Solo practice can succeed with a relatively small number of appointments per day.
- Group practice requires a consistently high daily volume.
- Concierge is viable at low volumes provided there are enough patients willing to enroll and pay the retainer.

We discussed the effect of different types of variability on realized capacity and its implications for appointment systems design in Chap. 4. Keeping that framework in mind, it helps to carry out the following in-class exercise. Think about management challenges that will arise for each type organizational structure in terms of patient experience, provider efficiency, costs and revenue, and work on developing separate lists for each model of practice. Examples of such lists are provided below.

Key Challenges for Group Practices

- Patient experience: budgeting the necessary amount of MD time, balancing of indirect and direct wait times, offering a large range of services, minimizing patients' out-of-pocket costs
- Provider efficiency: balancing idling and overtime while realizing high volume and high utilization
- Costs: staff (number, roles), customized EMR and IT systems, in-house diagnostic services
- Revenue: in-network fee negotiations with insurance, value-added services, revenue-cycle management

Key Challenges for Concierge Practices

- Patient experience: enabling direct or on-demand access to the MD, coordination of services needed by patients, convenience
- Provider efficiency: not a major concern, low volume, low utilization
- Costs: staff (number, roles), customized EMR and IT systems, negotiating priority access to ancillary services from other providers
- Revenue: initiation fee, annual retainer + monthly fees or visit-based cash payment, out of network for insurance, value-added services

Key Challenges for Solo Practices

- Patient experience: Direct MD access, a limited range of services, managing patients' expectations.
- Provider efficiency: Provider must balance multiple roles, low volume, high utilization.
- Costs: Limited or no staff, limited or use-based IT systems, ancillary services.
- Revenue: Cash payment, out of network for insurance.

These lists include concepts that have not been explained in detail in this book. This offers an opportunity to research (e.g., by utilizing AI tools) and discuss what terms like revenue-cycle management mean and options available to managers to deal with different types of variability. Student learning may be further enhanced by assigning specific readings and utilizing business cases to stimulate discussion.

Chapter 7
Clinic Appointment System Design

Two important and inter-related decisions that a clinic manager must make in collaboration with MDs, NPs, and other healthcare providers are target panel sizes and optimal appointment lengths. Panel sizes are an important measure of physician workload. They also determine clinic revenues. Appointment lengths must balance patient waiting on the one hand and physician idling on the other. Our goal in the next two sections is to learn some model-based approaches for thinking about how to make such decisions.

7.1 Optimal Panel Sizes

Panel size equals the count of patients who have declared a particular provider as their PCP.[1] Panel sizes affect (i) workload distribution among MDs, (ii) indirect wait times, and (iii) clinic revenue. The panel size and appointment length decisions are intertwined because larger panel sizes usually require more appointment slots per work day, and that in turn may put pressure on physicians to choose shorter appointment lengths. Shorter appointment lengths may cause an increase in direct waiting time for patients. That being said, panel size decisions are primarily affected by the concern for indirect wait times, i.e., the amount of delay that patients experience when they call to make an appointment. This delay is orders of magnitude greater than direct waiting time. Therefore, adding direct wait times to indirect wait times for the purpose of identifying optimal panel sizes will not make a significant difference to our calculations. For setting appointment lengths, we focus on direct wait times because the length of appointment slots is important for

[1] Note that not every clinic asks its patients to choose a particularly MD or NP as their primary care provider. Thus, panel size may be a loosely defined concept in those cases. It refers to the number of patients who frequently visit the same provider for their primary care needs.

D. Gupta, *Healthcare Analytics*, Springer Texts in Business and Economics,
https://doi.org/10.1007/978-3-032-24835-0_7

managing the in-clinic wait times—delays caused by previous patient's appointment not being finished prior to the start of the next appointment.

Let us consider how we may think about the relationship between panel sizes and patients' indirect wait times. Panel size affects the daily number of appointment requests that arise. In essence, the demand for appointments with a physician is greater if panel size is greater. Let λ (Greek letter lambda) denote the average daily number of appointment requests and μ (Greek letter mu) denote the average number of appointment slots that the physician has available each day. Depending on the current backlog, i.e., the number of patients whose appointments have been scheduled but have not occurred yet,[2] a patient who calls to make an appointment will need to wait a certain number of days before his or her request can be accommodated. Let the letter W_q denote the wait time of the patient (i.e., time in queue) and let W denote the sum of the waiting and service times of a patient. We argued earlier that W_q is often orders of magnitude greater than the in-clinic waiting time. Therefore, for the purpose of deciding panel sizes, one may treat them as being approximately the same, i.e., $W_q \approx W$.

W_q is the indirect wait time, and it depends on λ as well as μ. In general, $\lambda \leq \mu$ must hold; otherwise, the total demand will exceed capacity, and some patients will never be served unless they balk or renege or are removed from the queue by some other means. The wait time W_q is a random variable, and its value will vary from one patient to another. Let $E[W_q]$ denote the expected value of the random variable W_q. In this book, the notation $E[\cdot]$ stands for the expected value of the quantity within square brackets. A clinic manager may then choose a target panel size based on either (i) the expected wait time not exceeding a specified threshold, or (ii) the probability of W_q exceeding a particular threshold being at most a specified value. If the threshold is x, then the probability of interest is denoted as $P(W_q > x)$.

Why do we need two criteria? The two criteria address different aspects of patients' experience. Average wait times are a measure of patient experience in repeat interactions with the clinic's appointment system. Large wait times, in particular those that exceed a threshold x, represent instances of long wait times that may strongly influence a patient's perception of clinic's responsiveness to their needs. Thus, the two criteria capture different ways of thinking about patients' experience. Surprisingly, they may result in similar values of target panel sizes. Clinic managers calculate both $E[W_q]$ and $P(W_q > x)$, where x is the wait time threshold, and then adjust panel sizes until both performance metrics lie within their desirable ranges. In order to help clinic managers accomplish that task, we utilize mathematical expressions from queueing theory—see details in Sect. A.2.

In the jargon of queueing theory, each doctor is a server, appointment requests are customers, and the queue consists of the backlog of patients with future appointments who have not been served. A schematic of a queueing system with a single server is shown in Fig. 7.1.

In order to write mathematical expressions for $E[W]$ and $P(W > x)$, we define the following notation.

---

[2] In a typical appointment system, previously scheduled requests occupy earlier slots.

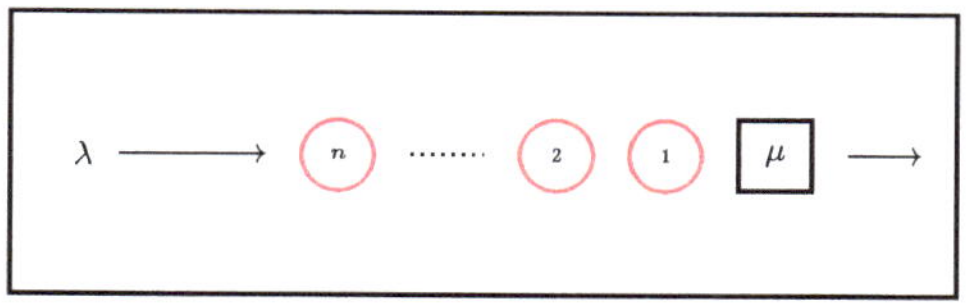

Fig. 7.1 A single server queue

$$E[L_q] = \text{average backlog or number of patients in the virtual queue}$$
$$E[W_q] = \text{average indirect waiting time}$$
$$E[L] = \text{average number in the system} = E[L_q] + \rho$$
$$E[W] = \text{average time in the system} = E[W_q] + E[S]$$
$$S = \text{service time, } E(S) = 1/\mu = \text{expected service time}$$
$$\rho = \lambda/\mu = \lambda E[S] = \text{ utilization}$$
$$C_\cdot^2 = \text{squared coefficient of variation} = \text{Var}(\cdot)/E[\cdot]^2$$
$$C_a^2 = \text{squared coefficient of variation of inter-arrival times}$$
$$C_S^2 = \text{squared coefficient of variation of service times } = \text{Var}(S)/E[S]^2$$

.

We assume the first-in-first-out service protocol and unlimited waiting room in the virtual queue of patients with appointments for future dates. Although the service protocol is not precisely first-in-first-out in healthcare settings, most patients generally book the earliest available future appointment. It can be shown that if arrivals are *Poisson*[3] and service times are *exponential*,[4] then

$$\text{Prob(Patient time-in-system } \leq x) = 1 - e^{-\mu(1-\rho)x}. \tag{7.1}$$

[3] The Poisson distribution is a distribution of count of events X. It specifies probability of number of events in time or space.

$$P_P(X = k) = \frac{e^{-m} m^k}{k!}, \qquad k \in \{0, 1, \cdots\}.$$

The term m is a parameter of the probability mass function (pmf) of X, i.e., $P_P(\cdot|m)$. Furthermore, $E[X] = m$ and $\text{Var}(X) = m$. Thus, the squared coefficient of variation of Poisson distributed X is $1/m$.

[4] The exponential distribution specifies the probability of elapsed time T (or space) between Poisson events.

$$f_E(t \mid m) = me^{-mt}, \qquad t \geq 0.$$

The term m is a parameter of the probability density function (pdf) of T, i.e., $f_E(\cdot|m)$. Furthermore, $E[T] = 1/m$ and $\text{Var}(T) = 1/m^2$. Thus, the squared coefficient of variation of exponentially distributed T is 1.

The above equation can also be written as

$$\begin{aligned}\text{Prob(Patient time-in-system } > x) &= 1 - \text{Prob(Patient time-in-system } \le x)\\ &= e^{-\mu(1-\rho)x}.\end{aligned} \tag{7.2}$$

Therefore, if we wanted to restrict the probability that the time in system would exceed x days to not exceed a threshold α, then we would set

$$e^{-\mu(1-\rho)x} = \alpha \Rightarrow \text{desired maximum } \lambda = \mu + \frac{\ln(\alpha)}{x}. \tag{7.3}$$

The above formula allows us to find the desired maximum arrival rate (demand rate) for each x and α. This expression is easy to use and often a good approximation even when arrivals are not Poisson and service times are not exponentially distributed. Similarly, $E[L]$ can be written as follows:

$$E[L] = E[L_q] + \rho, \tag{7.4}$$

where $E[L_q]$, the average number in the queue can be calculated using the following approximate formula:

$$E[L_q] \approx \left[\frac{(1 + C_s^2)(C_a^2 + \rho^2 C_s^2)}{1 + \rho^2 C_s^2}\right]\left(\frac{\rho^2}{2(1-\rho)}\right). \tag{7.5}$$

Equation (7.5) does not require Poisson arrivals and exponential service times assumptions. We write the formula in this form in order to separate the effect of variability from the effect of utilization, as much as possible. The first term within square brackets is the effect of variability of service and inter-arrival times, and the second term is the effect of utilization. Variability and utilization interact and magnify each others' effect on the number in the queue. The average number waiting and the average waiting time are related according to the following equation:

$$E[L] = \lambda E[W] \tag{7.6}$$

$$E[L_q] = \lambda E[W_q]. \tag{7.7}$$

Next, we shall work out two numerical examples to see how these concepts are applied.

Example 7.1 Consider a PCP with the current panel size of 1100. From the historical data, we find that she receives 15 appointment requests per day with $C_a^2 = 0.85$. Assume that the service time is constant at 20 minutes and that the physician's theoretical maximum capacity is 22 appointments per day:

- Calculate target panel size for this physician if the objective is to ensure that at most 5% of the patients wait more than 5 days.

- By how much will the target panel size change if the objective is to ensure that patients' average time in system (i.e., $E[W]$) does not exceed 5 days?

Answer Panel Size Calculations

Criterion 1

- Let r be the expected number of appointment requests per day per panel patient. Then, given λ arrivals per day and panel size N, r equals λ/N.
- From the data, historical $r = 15/1100 = 0.0136$. We assume that the MD attracts patients with similar clinical diversity. Therefore, r does not change upon changing the MD's panel size.
- Using (7.3), we have

$$\begin{aligned}\text{desired maximum } \lambda &= 22 + \frac{\ln(0.05)}{5} \\ &= 21.4.\end{aligned}$$

- Since r is not affected by changes to the panel size, we next calculate the desired $N = \frac{21.4}{.0136} = 1569.4$.
- The MD should aim to have about 1570 patients in her panel. Note that we rounded to the nearest integer.[5]

Criterion 2

- We observe that $C_a^2 \neq 1$ and $C_s^2 = 0$. The average wait time formula does not require that $C_a^2 = C_s^2 = 1$ should hold.
- Using the fact that $E[L] = \lambda E[W]$ or alternatively $E[L_q] = \lambda E[W_q]$ (see Appendix A.2), and setting $C_s^2 = 0$, we obtain the following equation,[6] which needs to be solved to get λ

$$E[W] = \frac{\lambda C_a^2}{2\mu(\mu - \lambda)} + \frac{1}{\mu} = 5.$$

Substitute the values of μ and C_a^2 and solve for λ to obtain:
- $\lambda = 21.91$. As before, since r does not change upon changing panel size, we obtain the desired $N = 1607.06$.

According to this calculation, the MD should aim to have a panel of about 1607 patients. Note that the estimates of desired panel sizes from the two criteria are close. This is not always true.

[5] Rounding should be deferred until the last step. If you round during intermediate steps, your results may not match those that are presented here.

[6] The steps needed to realize this simplification may be worked out in class.

Example 7.2 A primary care clinic manager has ascertained, using historical data, that in her clinic, the expected number of appointment requests per day per panel patient is approximately 0.02. She is interested in estimating target panel size for MDs who work two 4-hour sessions a day with a total of 16 appointment slots per day. The clinic manager has decided to choose panel sizes such that no more than 8% of the patients need to wait more than 6 days for an appointment. What is the target panel size?

Answer Here is how we may approach this problem. Relevant facts/data:

- $\alpha = 0.08$.
- $x = 6$.
- $\mu = 16$.
- $r = 0.02$.
- We need to find N:

- Using (7.3), we have

$$\begin{aligned}\text{desired maximum } \lambda &= 16 + \frac{\ln(0.08)}{6}\\ &= 15.579.\end{aligned}$$

- Therefore, $N = \frac{15.579}{.02} = 778.95$.

The clinic manager will likely set a target panel size of 779. In practice, these calculations serve to provide approximate targets. Therefore, in practice, the manager may round the calculated number to 780.

7.2 Optimal Appointment Lengths

In many situations, a manager needs to make a hedged decision in face of uncertainty—e.g., when choosing the length of an appointment slot, there are two types of costs to balance:

- The cost of having appointment lengths that are too long. Too long $\Rightarrow$ the physician will idle.
- The cost of having appointment lengths that are too short. Too short $\Rightarrow$ the next patient will be delayed.

How should the manager weigh these two competing priorities? Let us work this out. We introduce the following notation:

- x = appointment length (decision variable).
- Z = service time (random).

- $\max\{Z - x, 0\} = (Z - x)^+ =$ the amount that the next patient will wait.
- $\max\{x - Z, 0\} = (x - Z)^+ =$ the amount that the MD will idle.
- Objective: Choose x to minimize total cost, i.e., $\min_x\{c_u E[(Z-x)^+]+c_o E[(x-Z)^+]\}$.

In the above expression, the subscript u denotes underage and the subscript o denotes overage. With respect to the clinic manager's decision of choosing the appointment length, underage occurs when the next patient waits and overage occurs when the MD idles. Therefore, c_u is the cost of making the next patient wait per unit time, i.e., not enough appointment time, which is called underage, whereas c_o is the cost of idling the MD per unit time, i.e., too much appointment time, which is called overage. Therefore, $c_u E[(Z-x)^+]$ is the expected underage cost if there is a single appointment slot, and $c_o E[(x-Z)^+]$ is the expected overage cost. Usually, c_o is set much larger than c_u because group practices focus on maximizing revenue.

In the total cost expression, we add the expected underage and overage costs and then find the value of x that minimizes the total expected cost. The mathematical model we use to obtain a solution in situations like this is called the Newsvendor model—see details in Sect. A.1. The optimal solution is as follows:

$$x^* = F^{-1}\left(\frac{c_u}{c_u + c_o}\right),$$

where $F(\cdot)$ is the cumulative distribution function (CDF) of Z, the patient's service time, and the fraction $\frac{c_u}{c_u+c_o}$ is called the critical ratio. The above model is only approximately appropriate for setting appointment lengths because delays accumulate for patients whose appointments are later in the day. Still, the model provides a useful way to think about setting appointment lengths because it captures the key trade-off and it is easy to use. We consider two examples next.

Example 7.3 Suppose a patient's service time is uniformly distributed between 15 and 25 minutes, $c_o = 1.5$ and $c_u = 0.5$. What should the clinic set as the appointment length?

Answer

- Because the service time is uniformly distributed, we have $F(z) = \frac{z-15}{25-15} = \frac{z-15}{10}$ for $15 \le z \le 25$. $F(z) = 0$ for $z < 15$ and $F(z) = 1$ for $z > 25$.
- The critical ratio is $\frac{0.5}{1.5+.5} = 0.25$.
- This means $x^* = x : \frac{x-15}{10} = .25$, which implies $x^* = 17.5$ minutes.
- In practice, the clinic will likely choose 20 minutes because of the practical challenge of utilizing appointment lengths that are not in increments of 5 minutes.
- You may wonder whether the clinic should ever round down in cases where the calculated value was, say, 17.2 minutes as an example. That is, should the clinic use 15 minutes in such cases? The answer is no because that will be equivalent to using an even lower underage cost, which is typically set lower than the overage cost by the clinic managers to begin with.

Example 7.4 A healthcare analyst hired by a primary care clinic is tasked with finding the optimal length of appointment slots. The analyst obtains historical data from past appointments and finds that actual appointment lengths are approximately exponentially distributed with parameter m such that the average appointment length equals $1/m = 20$ minutes. It was difficult to get agreement on the consequences of not scheduling enough time, although MDs agreed that they would strongly prefer not to have excessive idle time between appointments. After conducting a few interviews, the analyst concludes that the cost of having shorter than needed appointment slots, which results in patient waiting, could be reasonably estimated to be 3/4 of the cost of idling the doctors. What should the analyst recommend to the clinic manager?

Answer Here is how we may approach the problem. This is what we know:

- $\text{Prob}(T \leq t) = F(t) = 1 - e^{-mt}$, for any $t \geq 0$, where T denotes the random duration of an arbitrary appointment. We also know that $m = 1/20$.
- Let the cost of overage $c_o = 1$. Then, the cost of underage, i.e., cost of having a shorter than needed appointment slot $= c_u = 3/4$.
- Critical ratio $= \frac{0.75}{1.75} = 0.43$.

Let t^* denote the optimal appointment slot length. Then, we need to solve the following equation:

$$F(t^*) = 1 - e^{-t^*/20} = 0.43 \tag{7.8}$$

$$\Leftrightarrow e^{-t^*/20} = 0.57 \tag{7.9}$$

$$\Leftrightarrow t^* = -\ln(0.57) * 20 \tag{7.10}$$

$$= 11.19. \tag{7.11}$$

From above calculations, the optimal appointment length is 11.2 minutes. However, if this were a real example, the clinic manager would round this number to 15. Therefore, the analyst should recommend 15-minute-long appointment slots.

7.3 Same-Day Appointments Paradigm

You may have surmised that faster access and provider efficiency are often at odds, i.e., higher efficiency leads to longer indirect wait times. Some clinics have experimented with the concept of providing same-day appointments. You will encounter this concept in a short case at the end of this book. The case is titled Eagle Health, Inc. (A)—see Chap. 14. This situation described in this case arose as a result of an experiment conducted by a multi-clinic health system to gain competitive advantage by offering patients access to physicians on a same-day basis. The need for exploring such strategies stems in part from the fact that wait times are the number one cause of patient dissatisfaction in the outpatient setting. Also, thought leaders in the healthcare operations field had proposed the idea that clinics should be able to meet each day's demand on the same day by flexing capacity. The idea originated from the observation that for many clinics, the daily average number of appointment requests are no more than the daily number of appointment slots available (Murray & Berwick, 2003). This is of course true because in the long run patients must be able to book appointments, or else they will find alternate service providers.

The same-day appointments paradigm (also known as an advanced access system), required physicians to change capacity (recall that we labeled a more general form of this strategy as synchronized variability) such that most patients could obtain an appointment within 24 hours of their call. Unfortunately, the implementation of the strategy also resulted in some unintended consequences, which you will be able to appreciate upon performing an analysis of the data accompanying the Eagle Health, Inc. (A) case. Some of these issues will be discussed in detail when your class discusses the Eagle Health, Inc. (A) case.

Chapter 8
Exercises for Part II

8.1 Discussion Questions

In each of the following cases, choose the appropriate operational and revenue model for each block.

Case 1

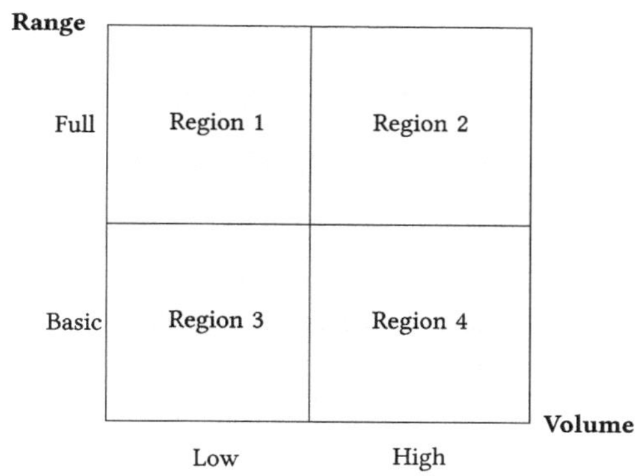

Range refers to the range of services offered, and volume refers to the number of patients registered with the practice.

D. Gupta, *Healthcare Analytics*, Springer Texts in Business and Economics,
https://doi.org/10.1007/978-3-032-24835-0_8

Case 2

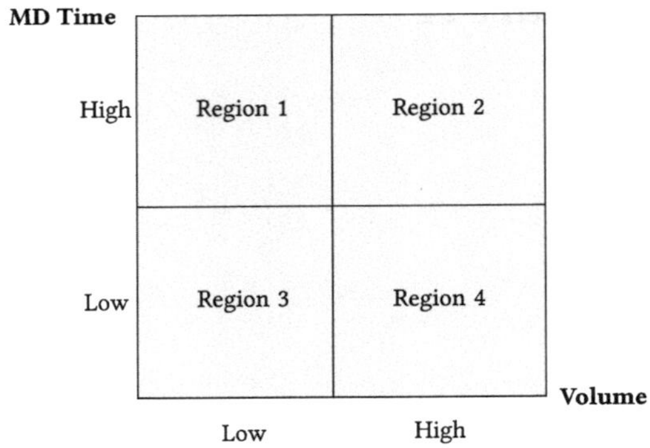

MD time refers to the amount of time that MD has available to attend to each patient, and volume refers to the number of patients registered with the practice. Often, the appointment length is used as a proxy for MD time.

8.2 Multiple-Choice Questions

1. What does the term PCP mean? Check all that apply:
   - Any MD who has been selected as the preferred provider by at least one patient
   - Any primary care provider
   - For each patient visit, the MD that the patient consulted
   - A MD who sees the largest daily number of patients on average
   - A MD who works full time
2. Why should a clinic pay attention to MD panel sizes? Check all that apply:
   - To ensure fair allocation of workload
   - To realize the full revenue potential
   - To balance patient indirect wait times and clinic revenue
   - To minimize spoilage
   - To maintain in-network status with regional insurers
3. Which of the following factors could help lower no show and late cancelation rates? Check all that apply:
   - Appointment reminders (call, email, postcard).
   - Appointment overbooking.
   - Offering same-day appointments.
   - Not allowing patients to book appointments too far in advance.
   - Making sure patients, see their PCPs.

4. Which of the following symptoms might suggest that a clinic has not optimized its appointments management system? Check all that apply:

- Long direct wait times
- Patient dissatisfaction
- MDs and staff having to work overtime
- Low spoilage rate
- High PCP match

5. In Eagle Health (A), what were the primary concerns of the MDs? Check all that apply:

- Patients were waiting too long for appointments.
- Patients did not care about seeing their PCP.
- Some doctors filled up all of their appointment slots with their panel patients.
- The spoilage rate was high.
- The strategy of offering same-day appointments led to lower PCP match.

8.3 Long-Answer Questions

Problem 8.1 A hospital system needs to decide how many life-saving machines to purchase (order quantity) before knowing the demand for them. The cost of an life-saving machine is $250,000. The hospital determined that the imputed cost of not meeting patients' need is $400,000 per MRI machine short (net of the cost of machine itself):

1. What is the optimal order quantity of life-saving machines if demand follows a Normal distribution with mean 5000 and standard deviation 1000?
2. The hospital gathered some historical data on the need for life-saving machines each week, as shown in the table below.

Demand	Relative frequency
3000	0.01
3200	0.12
3500	0.07
4000	0.29
4600	0.27
6000	0.15
6100	0.09

What is the optimal order quantity in this case?

3. How would your answer to the previous question change if \$400,000 were the cost of expedited ordering of a life-saving machine, instead of the imputed cost of not meeting patients' need?

Problem 8.2 A PCP has a current panel size of 1200 patients. From historical data, she finds that she receives 12 appointment requests per day, with $C_a^2 = 0.9$. Assume that service time is constant at 25 minutes and that the physician's theoretical maximum capacity is 18 appointments per day. What is the PCP's target panel size if the objective is to ensure that patients' average time in the system does not exceed 6 days?

Part III
Hospital Operations

Chapter 9
Introduction

According to the American Hospital Association, in 2022, there were 6093 hospitals in the USA with 920,531 staffed beds and total expenditures in excess of $1.1 trillion (see fact sheet at https://www.aha.org/statistics/fast-facts-us-hospitals). The size of a hospital is often described in terms of the number of acute care beds it has. There are three building blocks of a hospital—emergency department (ED), operating rooms (ORs), and inpatient units. The latter are further divided into different levels of care and different clinical foci. Broadly speaking, there are three levels of care—intensive care (highest) level, step-down (intermediate) level, and medical-surgical (general) level. However, there may also exist clinical foci. For example, ICUs could be specialized for surgical, cardiac, neonatal, and pediatric patients. For administrative convenience and sometimes space constraints, each level of care and clinical specialty may have multiple units. These may even be on different floors of the hospital. Each unit, also referred to as a hospital ward, is managed by a nurse administrator who is sometimes referred to as the *health unit coordinator* or HUC nurse. A typical unit has 10 to 30 beds.

The in- and outflow of patients through a typical hospital is shown in the schematic in Fig. 9.1. All patients are admitted first before being able to access inpatient beds. Exceptions to this rule are patients seen in the ED that are discharged without being admitted, and day-surgery cases. The latter refers to cases involving relatively minor surgeries after which patients are sent home to recover. Some hospitals run stand-alone day-surgery centers with few or no inpatient beds. They have agreements in place with area hospitals that have inpatient beds to accommodate those patients that may need extended care. Similar to this trend, one finds stand-alone emergency centers in many metropolitan areas. These facilities are similar to urgent care clinics. They are staffed by Emergency Room doctors and typically have no inpatient beds. They are able to bill insurance at the rate that hospital-based EDs do, but they do not incur the costs associated with maintaining inpatient beds.

D. Gupta, *Healthcare Analytics*, Springer Texts in Business and Economics,
https://doi.org/10.1007/978-3-032-24835-0_9

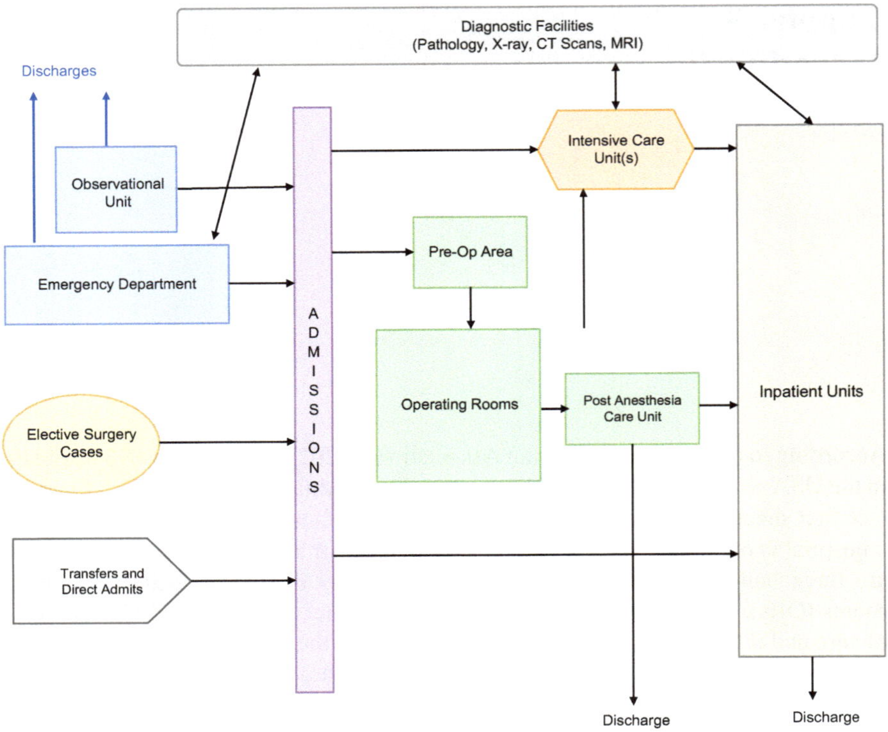

Fig. 9.1 Typical patient flow in hospitals

Demand for inpatient beds can arise from EDs, ORs, direct admits, and transfers. The ED demand is random and generally thought to be more variable. However, without careful management, demand for inpatient beds coming from operating rooms can be just as variable and sometimes more variable. Many hospitals have extensive diagnostic and laboratory capabilities, e.g., X-ray, MRI, pathology lab, etc. Some hospitals also include pharmacies. In addition, most hospitals run cafeteria, coffee shops, and gift shops for family members and visitors of admitted patients. Once admitted to an inpatient bed, patient recovery times are often highly variable. Recovery time is referred to as the length of stay (LOS). This variability gives rise to the challenge of matching supply and demand for hospital services (see Gupta & Potthoff, 2016 for further details). It is not uncommon to utilize patients' average length of stay (ALOS) by patient type as an aggregate metric of hospital care needs of patients of that type. We focus in this chapter on how hospital managers may leverage data and operations management tools to balance supply and demand in a cost-effective manner.

9.1 The USA Versus The OECD

We begin by comparing ALOS across all patient types per 100,000 population in the USA versus selected OECD countries in Fig. 9.2. This graph shows that ALOS is nearly at the bottom among US hospitals. This can be explained by the DRG-based system of paying hospitals introduced by the CMS in mid-1980s and later adopted by private insurers as well. According to this system, hospital stays are divided into discharge codes, known as diagnosis-related groups (DRGs). For each patient discharged, the hospital must identify an appropriate DRG as the primary reason for the hospitalization. Payments to the hospitals are based on the DRG, irrespective of the LOS and incurred cost. The payments are adjusted for patients' comorbidity, hospital status as a teaching hospital, disproportionate share of uninsured care, and local economic environment (additional details can be found at https://www.cms.gov/medicare/payment/prospective-payment-systems/acute-inpatient-pps). The payment system that the CMS adopted is known as the inpatient prospective payment system (IPPS).

Can you construct arguments explaining why US hospitals chose to reduce LOS in response to the IPPS? A discussion is provided at the end of this chapter in Sect. 9.7.

A comparison of bed utilization in Fig. 9.3, however, shows that US utilization of beds is not as high as that in other countries. In order to understand why, we need to look at the difference between licensed beds and staffed beds. US hospitals typically have many more licensed beds. They do not staff all of them all the time. Rather staffing levels are adjusted to match supply with demand. In developing national-

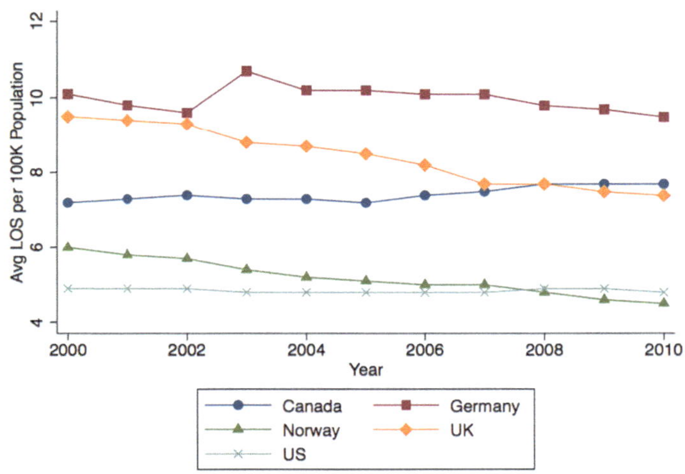

Fig. 9.2 Average LOS, USA versus selected OECD countries

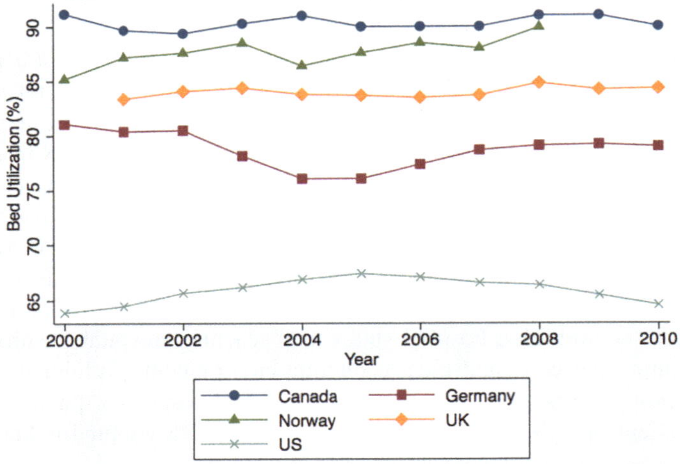

Fig. 9.3 Average bed utilization, USA versus selected OECD countries

level bed utilization statistics, often the denominator is the number of licensed beds. Therefore, bed utilization appears to be lower in the USA, even though shortage of staffed beds is a common phenomenon.

9.2 A Hospital Manager's Challenges

A significant challenge that hospital operations managers face is how to cope with variability. Fortunately, not all variability is random. There are distinct patterns that can be leveraged to design coping strategies. For the purpose of understanding different types of variability, it is useful to group them into three categories—demand variability, processing time variability, and protocol variability. The first is straightforward to explain. Demand for ED services, surgeries, and hospital beds varies by time of day and day of week. There may also be seasonal patterns, e.g., demand for certain types of beds may be higher during the flu season. A key driver of operational costs is the peaks in demand. Flattening the peak demand helps smooth resource requirements (in particular, staffing), leading to efficient operations and reduced staff burnout. While the variability in certain types of demand, e.g., ED, cannot be controlled, it is possible to exercise a certain degree of control over some other types of demand, e.g., elective surgeries. Natural variability of demand (random or according to a predictable pattern) interacts with resource management practices to produce utilization peaks and bottlenecks. Therefore, understanding rhythms of demand variability are important for thinking about good management practices.

Different patients may take different amounts of time to recover even after controlling for the care provided by the hospital. Similarly, surgical procedure times may vary from one patient to another depending on patient physiology and comorbidity even after controlling for other factors such as physician expertise. Processing time variability refers to the natural variability that exists in treatment and healing processes. This is often manifest in the surgery duration and patients' lengths of stay (LOS). However, when examining data, one must consider endogeneity caused by operational factors. For example, doctors in charge of issuing discharge orders may use different discharge criteria when the bed occupancy is high as compared to when it is not. As analysts, we often do not observe all the factors that affect the clinicians' judgment and how.

The Healthcare Cost and Utilization Project of the Agency for Healthcare Research and Quality is a good source of data for students and instructors interested in national-level or state-level data on inpatient, ambulatory surgery, and emergency department volumes (https://hcup-us.ahrq.gov/databases.jsp). The data are not free, but there exists a free data visualization tool that can be used for demonstration purposes.

Finally, there is protocol variability, which refers to variability in clinical practice (treatment or other prescribed interventions) across providers. Sometimes such variability results from an effort to customize treatment to patients' needs. However, in many instances, the variability stems from treatment preferences of the providers, who may be exposed to different approaches for treating similar clinical symptoms during their medical training. On the one hand, protocol variability can lead to higher costs and inconsistent clinical outcomes. On the other hand, outcomes data associated with such variability can be leveraged to identify tailored treatment protocols for specific types of patients and improve care guidelines.

In what follows, let us examine visualizations of sample data from hospitals in aggregate form.

9.2.1 Examples of Variability

Demand variability can be visualized by plotting the number of admissions and discharges to all step-down units of a medium-sized hospital by time of day (ToD) and the variability in the number of patients who arrive at the ED by ToD. Figure 9.4 shows the pattern of admissions and discharges, and Fig. 9.5 shows the pattern for ED arrivals. Note that in Fig. 9.4 admissions could be from ED, OR, transfers, or direct admits. The ED arrival variability is censored data because if a patient leaves without registering at the front desk, then hospitals do not have a record of that arrival.

The labels on the horizontal axis in Fig. 9.4 are constructed as follows: "0" means arrivals during midnight and 1 a.m., 1 means arrivals during 1 and 2 a.m., and so on until 23 means arrivals during 11 p.m. and midnight. Note that the count of admissions is nearly constant between 10 a.m. and 7 p.m. It falls off after 7 p.m.

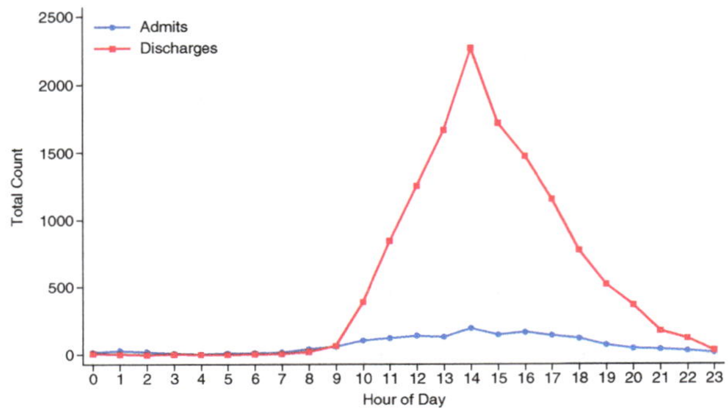

Fig. 9.4 Admissions and discharges by time of day

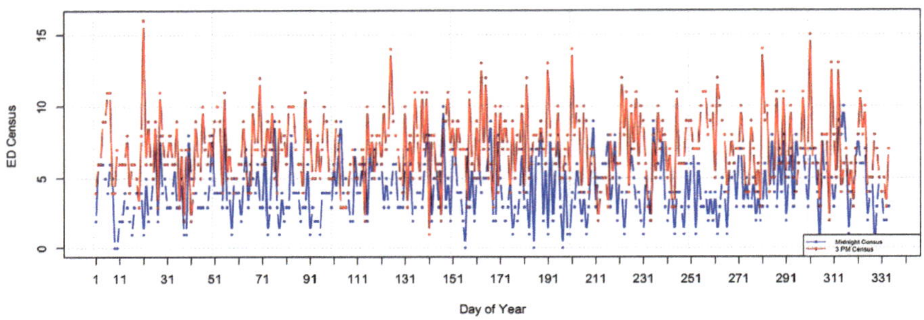

Fig. 9.5 Hourly ED arrivals 12–1 a.m. and 3–4 p.m.; 11-month data from a 400-bed community hospital

and remains at a nearly zero level after 11 p.m. until about 7 a.m., after which the admissions' counts start to rise. Note that even when admissions count is zero, the number of beds occupied in these units is not zero. In contrast, the count of discharges shows a distinct ToD peak, which occurs at 2 p.m. Although this pattern is from a single hospital, similar pattern is also observed at many other hospitals.

The number of admissions is fairly steady during the day because of the circadian rhythm. At night, only a few ORs are open and overall activity level of the population declines. Therefore, arrivals to the hospital decline between the hours of 10 p.m. and 5 a.m. The contrasting nature of counts of discharges is explained by the common practice of making discharge decisions after surgeons (or hospitalists) have completed their rounds. At the start of the day, the hospital staff is occupied with getting the day's operations underway. Rounds do not complete until late morning or early afternoon. It takes some time to prepare patients for discharge. Late morning and early afternoon are also the times when the demand for hospital beds starts to build up because morning surgery patients need to be moved out of the Post Anesthesia Care Unit (PACU) to the wards. Discharges are therefore prioritized because of the high demand for beds. While this practice is common, it also leads to uneven staff workload and creates the potential for small variations causing relatively large backlog of patients in need of hospital beds.

There is also a weekly cycle of bed census that can be explained by the daily admission-discharge cycles and OR schedules. Each day, patient census builds up until about 3 p.m. and then declines. There is also a day-of-week (DoW) pattern. There is a buildup of daily peaks from Monday to Friday because admitted patients take several days to heal. The peaks are relatively smaller on Saturdays and Sundays. This happens because hospitals do not perform deferrable (elective) surgeries during the weekend. Admissions from OR suites account for 40–50% of admissions in hospitals. Therefore, fewer hospital beds are occupied over the weekend. The reason why peaks build up is that surgery patients take a few days to recover. For example, patients who are admitted on Monday may not be discharged until Thursday. Thus, each day of additional surgeries adds to the buildup of census. There are relatively fewer surgeries performed on Fridays.

Figure 9.6 shows the number of staffed ORs (in response to demand for surgeries) at a rural hospital with 10 ORs on different days of the week. Note that this figure shows the number of ORs that were staffed, and not the demand for surgeries. If there is insufficient capacity on a particular day, surgeries may get postponed or moved to another hospital. Thus, underlying Fig. 9.6 is censored demand for ORs.

The data are summarized as box-and-whisker plots by weekday with "1" representing Monday and "5" representing Friday. This hospital did not operate ORs during weekends. Observe that the median number of ORs that this hospital operates is 9 on Mondays and Wednesdays, but drops to 8 on Tuesdays, Thursdays, and Fridays. Moreover, the number of staffed ORs shows significant dips on Mondays. This is in part due to the fact that several statutory holidays fall on Mondays.

Inpatient beds are typically grouped into wards or inpatient units. Each unit is ideally suited for providing care to patients with specific diagnoses. Examples of

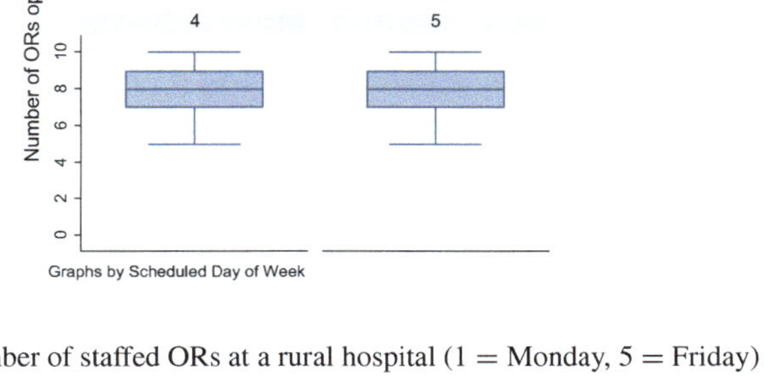

Fig. 9.6 Number of staffed ORs at a rural hospital (1 = Monday, 5 = Friday)

inpatient units include intensive care units, pediatric units, neonatal units, maternity units, neurological units, orthopedic units, surgical units, and medical-surgical units. Each unit has a cohort of nurses who routinely work in that unit. Almost all inpatient units operate 24 hours a day, seven days a week. This requires careful planning of nurse shift assignments. The assignments are guided by accepted norms regarding how many patients may be assigned to a nurse in a single shift, referred to as the nurse-to-patient (N:P) ratio. Assignment of patients to nurses is further informed by the need to maintain familiarity with the needs of the patients that each nurse cares for. Whereas nurses typically prefer to know their work schedules well in advance, unit managers try to adjust staffing to match availability of nurses with the changing bed census. Census is affected by the number of admissions, discharges, and transfers in and out of each unit. Variability in census is different across different units. It is often the cause of imbalances in available nursing care and care requirements, which leads to the use of overtime and agency (temporary) nurses. Many hospitals therefore track bed census and nurse to patient ratios, actual and target values, on a daily, weekly, and monthly basis. An example of variability of census of an inpatient unit is shown in Fig. 9.7. This plot is censored by the availability of staffed beds because patients are not admitted when the unit capacity is exceeded. Figure 9.7 shows census at midnight, 10 a.m. and 8 p.m. The hospital has shift changes at 11 p.m., 7 a.m., and 3 p.m. Note that the variability exhibited in Fig. 9.7 is caused not only by changing requirements for inpatient beds and variable

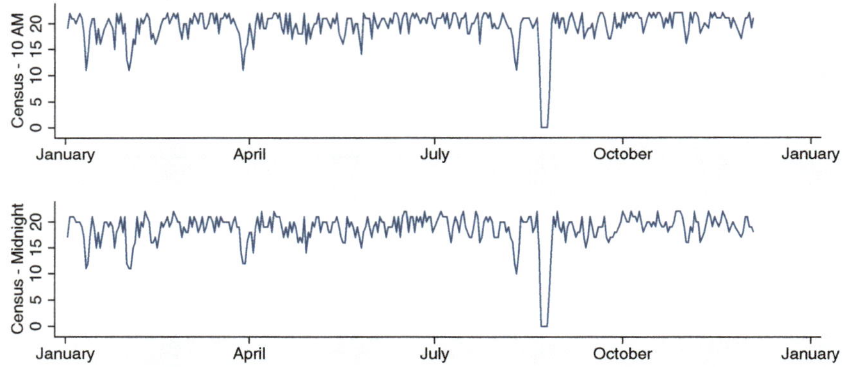

Fig. 9.7 22-bed inpatient unit census variability (censored)

lengths of stay, but also by the hospital's bed management practices, i.e., how beds are assigned to patients, and timing of discharge of recovered patients.

9.3 Hospital Customer-Service Models

Hospitals may choose to be either general hospitals, which means that they do not specialize in the care of any particular patient population or particular diagnoses, or specialty hospitals. The latter specialize in the care of particular patient populations, e.g., children's hospitals, or particular clinical diagnoses such as cancer treatment. Some hospitals specialize in certain types of surgical procedures, e.g., cardiac hospitals that specialize in heart surgeries. Many specialty hospitals also provide general care on a limited basis. However, they use their specialty status to attract patients. Furthermore, certain specialties are exempt from the IPPS payment regime, that is, certain specialty hospitals can still charge CMS on an FFS basis. Details of such exemptions can be found by visiting the following web page: https://www.cms.gov/Outreach-and-Education/Medicare-Learning-Network-MLN/MLNProducts/html/medicare-payment-systems.html.

9.4 Hospital Operations Strategy Paradigms

While each hospital customizes its operations strategy to suit its particular circumstances, it is instructive to group these strategies into two categories, based on the key management focus. These are (1) asset focused and (2) disease (or service line) focused. Examples of assets are MDs and nurses who work at the hospital, diagnostic labs and imaging equipment and personnel, operating rooms (ORs), and ICU beds. Similarly, examples of service lines are cardiovascular care, respiratory care, and orthopedic care. With the latter focus, a hospital organizes its resources to provide seamless and efficient care for groups of patients with similar care needs. Invariably, this requires management to exercise oversight over clinical practices in order to measure, standardize, and improve clinical outcomes. In contrast, when the focus is on assets, the hospital management attempts to maximize resource utilization and efficiency. Management views clinical practice as the domain of medical professionals. Key differences between asset-focused and disease-focused management paradigms can be summarized as follows.

Asset Focused

- Optimize use of assets employed in care delivery.
- Leave clinical protocols to medical professionals.
- Reduce service-time variability.
- Manage demand and flow.

Disease (Service Line) Focused

- Measure clinical processes (inputs and outputs).
- Control processes of care for groups of patients who interact with the delivery system at multiple point.
- Standardize, but allow variation, learn from the unusual.

It is useful at this juncture to discuss the pros and cons of each approach. It is also useful to debate which approach is more prevalent among US hospitals and why? A discussion is provided at the end of this chapter in Sect. 9.8.

9.5 Hospital Revenue Models

Most hospitals receive payments from patients' insurance companies. CMS is a major payer because among those who need hospital care, many are elderly. Like outpatient clinics, hospitals too were historically paid on the basis of the volume of services provided. For ease of understanding, it is reasonable to think of the historical payment regime as a per-diem method of paying hospitals, i.e., for each day of hospital stay. In addition, hospitals also billed for medications and any unusual services provided. This changed with the introduction of the DRG-based payment system introduced by the CMS in 1984 and since then widely adopted by all payers. DRG stands for diagnosis-related group. It is a system of grouping primary reasons for hospitalization into groups based on clinical similarity. A DRG-based payment system pays hospitals a fixed sum, after adjusting for severity, regional differences (rural, urban, labor costs), and the percent of uninsured patients that the hospital cares for. However, the payment does not depend on the actual number of days of hospitalization.

Similar to changes in the payment regime for outpatient clinics, hospitals may be incentivized to provide care for a population of patients and receive payments that are measured against a budget. Typically, cost savings relative to the budget are shared between the payer and the hospital provided the hospital meets specified quality standards. There are two different approaches that have emerged in this context—the bundled payment method and the capitation-based method. Both are examples of VBPs and are targeted at provider groups (hereafter health systems) rather than stand-alone hospitals. The former makes the health system accountable for all services required to provide care for a particular episode of care, e.g., lower extremity joint replacement. The latter makes the health system responsible all care needs (in- and outpatient) for a population of patients. The health system may face both upside and downside risks.[1] Such health systems are also known as Accountable Care Organizations (ACOs).

[1] Optional: Students interested in a summary of developments in this arena and their impact are encouraged to read Song (2019).

It may be useful at this point to think about how a hospital's chief financial officer may respond to a change from DRG to value-based payment regime. When developing these ideas, students may benefit from reading the following articles James and Poulsen (2016) and Porter and Kaplan (2016).

9.6 Regulatory Landscape

Payers (insurers), health systems, and healthcare providers are highly regulated in the USA. The regulations are intended to protect consumers (patients), providers, and payers of healthcare. However, they also create some unintended consequences. Some of the operationally important provisions are as follows:

1. The *Emergency Medical Treatment and Labor Act (EMTALA)*, 1986
2. The Social Security Act: Sections [1128A(b)(1)-(2)], 1999, *Civil Monetary Penalty (CMP)* for a hospital
3. The Social Security Act:[Section 1128(b)], 1972, *Anti-kickback statute*
4. The *Stark law*, 1989, or *The Physician Self-referral Law*

In lay person terms, these laws can be explained as follows:

- EMTALA requires Medicare-participating hospitals (i.e., hospitals that receive reimbursement from CMS) with emergency departments to screen and treat the emergency medical conditions of patients in a nondiscriminatory manner to anyone, regardless of their ability to pay, insurance status, national origin, race, creed, or color.
- CMP says that physicians may not be induced to reduce or limit services provided to patients. On the one hand, this law protects the patients and the providers. On the other hand, it can limit hospitals' efforts to implement cost-effective clinical practices because physicians may not be rewarded or punished for their choice of treatment although each treatment choice may have different implications on a hospital's cost.
- The anti-kickback statute states that no one may offer, pay, solicit, or receive payment to induce or reward referrals. It implies that hospitals may neither receive nor give referral-based incentives.
- The Stark law states that physicians may not refer patients to a facility with which they have a financial relationship. It implies that the choice of treatment must be based on medical, not financial, considerations. In a VBP regime, health systems benefit from keeping all patient care within their network. When patients receive service from an out-of-network provider, health systems have to pay that provider on an FFS basis, even though they receive a fixed payment per enrollee, typically on a per-member per-month (PMPM) basis. Therefore, they tend to refer patients to within-network providers. The phenomenon of patients seeking services of a provider outside the health network is also referred to as "leakage." To the extent that encouraging physicians to refer patients to other within-network specialists

may be viewed as encouraging self-referrals, such practices by hospitals may violate the Stark Law.

A detailed description of the three building blocks of hospitals, i.e., EDs, ORs, and inpatient units, is provided in Chaps. 10, 11, and 12 of this book (also see Gupta & Potthoff, 2016).

9.7 DRG-Based Payments and LOS

The impact of DRG-based payment scheme on a hospital can be explained by utilizing the Little's Law—recall equation 4.1. For this purpose, we interpret the various parts of Eq. (4.1) as follows:

1. Backlog = the average number of patients in beds, i.e., the average number of occupied beds.
2. Arrival rate = the average discharge rate of patients.
3. Time in system = average LOS.

Some patients are unable to access hospital services when beds are not available. Therefore, the demand for hospital services (effective arrival rate) is the discharge rate of patients. The demand rate and consequently the discharge rate are determined by the medical needs of the population served by the hospital. Hospitals have little control over them. Under the FFS scheme, hospitals were paid on the basis of LOS (per-diem payments). Suppose the hospital's cost per day of hospital stay is fixed and at least slightly smaller than the revenue per day. Then, by maintaining LOS high, hospitals earned more net revenue, which could help to pay their fixed costs as well as contribute to net profit. Keep in mind that hospitals decide when to discharge patients, i.e., the LOS.

After the DRG payments were implemented, hospitals received a fixed payment for each discharge. The payment varied by DRG, but not by LOS. However, their costs were still proportional to the LOS, and they still needed sufficient revenue to pay the fixed costs. Given that discharge rates were relatively fixed, this left only one lever available to the hospitals—lower their costs by affecting LOS. The balance between backlog, discharge rate, and LOS is still maintained, but with lower backlog and lower LOS. That means fewer beds would be occupied on average.

The hospitals have an incentive to not staff all their beds and match staffing (which is a large component of their operating costs) to census, while at the same time lower LOS. The trade-offs are further complicated by the Certificate of Need (CON) programs implemented by 35 out of 50 states and Washington, DC.[2] These programs require hospitals to obtain approval from a health planning agency or other entity prior to creating new facilities or expanding existing facilities

[2] See https://nashp.org/state-tracker/50-state-scan-of-state-certificate-of-need-programs/

(including beds). Therefore, hospitals have tended to maintain their historical bed count (referred to as the number of licensed beds), but not staff all of them all of the time. A positive consequence of this development is the availability of surge capacity when demand peaks occur, e.g., during the Covid-19 pandemic. This may also explain lower reported values of bed utilization rates in the USA compared to other OECD countries (see Fig. 9.3).

9.8 Differences Between Asset- and Disease-Focused Approaches

The asset- and disease-focused approaches are not mutually exclusive. They may be practiced at the same time. For example, a hospital may have service lines organized by categories of diseases for which patients require similar hospital resources for treatment, and at the same time, focus on maximizing efficiency of assets assigned to each service line. However, there are some differences.

A disease-focused approach requires the hospital to develop standardized clinical pathways and treatment protocols for diagnoses comprising the majority of its patients. This can be both time-consuming and contentious. Different health professionals may have different opinions about which standardized approach is best. It requires hospital management to develop a culture of evidence-based practice and to continually evolve its protocols as clinical knowledge evolves. For many hospitals, this can be a daunting task. In addition, management must provide clinicians information about the cost and quality of the interventions and treatments they choose.

In contrast, asset-focused approach utilizes efficiency metrics that are often well known to professional managers. For example, utilization rates of ORs, MRI machines, and ICU beds, and nurse-to-patient ratios. Such statistics can be used to fine-tune patient flow and to determine the number of resources needed to strike a balance between efficiency and patient wait times. An asset-focused approach may also pay attention to the results of patient satisfaction surveys. It may use a strategy of training medical professionals in accounting principles and hiring highly regarded health professionals (e.g., MDs) to ensure superior clinical outcomes.

Chapter 10
Managing ED Operations

10.1 Patient Flow

The typical patient flow through an ED is as depicted in Fig. 10.1. The ED length of stay has three distinct components: arrival to first-provider contact, first-provider contact to disposition decision, and disposition decision to departure. The departure could mean either discharge or admission to the hospital. If no hospital bed is available, then the patient may be boarded in the ED.

In what follows, we discuss processes that occur in each block comprising ED length of stay.

10.2 Arrival to First-Provider Contact

When patients arrive/register/check in at an ED, either on their own, or via ambulance, they are triaged (classified) into one of five categories based on the urgency of their needs. These categories are called *emergency severity index (ESI)* levels. The five levels are described in Table 10.1. After triage, patients are either taken immediately to a treatment room or to a waiting area from which they go to the treatment room when their turn arrives, where the first-provider contact occurs. Providers are typically MDs, but may also include NPs, or MD assistants.

A schematic of the workflow until first-provider contact is shown in Fig. 10.2.

10.3 First-Provider Contact to Disposition

The first provider that patients typically encounter is an emergency room doctor (MD). The MD after conducting patient interview determines if tests are required to

D. Gupta, *Healthcare Analytics*, Springer Texts in Business and Economics,
https://doi.org/10.1007/978-3-032-24835-0_10

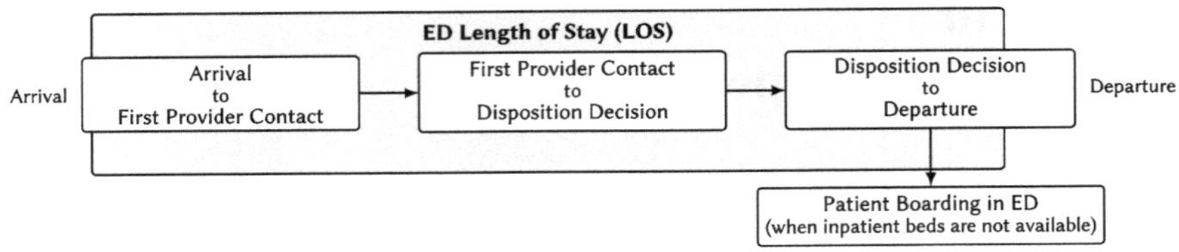

Fig. 10.1 Patient flow through an ED

Table 10.1 Common emergency severity index levels

ESI level	Description
ESI level 1	Patient requires immediate life-saving intervention (1–3% of all ED patients)
ESI level 2	Patient is in a high-risk situation or is confused/lethargic/disoriented or is in severe pain/distress and should not wait to be seen (20–30% of all ED patients)
ESI level 3	Patient is not level 1 or level 2, has vital signs within the accepted range for the patient's age, and is predicted to require two or more resources, such as labs, diagnostic testing, intravenous fluids, intravenous, intramuscular or nebulized medications, specialty consultation, and/or a simple procedure or complex procedure (30–40% of all ED patients)
ESI level 4	Patient has vital signs within the accepted range for the patient's age, and is predicted to use one resource (combined with ESI level 5 is 20–35% of all ED patients, and is an appropriate level to stream through fast-track)
ESI level 5	Patient has vital signs within the accepted range for the patient's age, and is predicted to require no resource (combined with ESI level 4 is 20–35% of all ED patients, and is an appropriate level to stream through fast-track)

complete patient diagnosis and treatment plan. If tests are needed, then the patient is typically sent to a different part of the hospital where diagnostic imaging and laboratory facilities are housed. Patients have to be transported back and forth to the testing facility and wait for the results of their tests to be reported back to the MD. After test results are received, the MD arrives at a diagnosis and appropriate treatment plan. The latter may involve hospitalization. This is referred to as the ED physician disposition decision.

A schematic of the workflow until first-provider contact is shown in Fig. 10.3.

10.4 Disposition to Discharge

After the disposition decision, patients split into two streams—those that will be admitted to the hospital and those that will be discharged to their homes. For the former, the ER doctor issues an inpatient bed request and then hands over the patients needing inpatient beds to an admitting physician. The latter

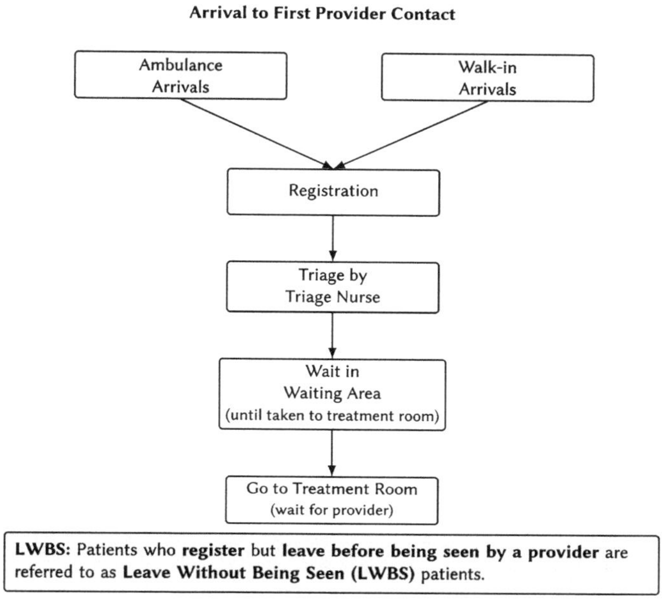

Fig. 10.2 Arrival to first-provider contact workflow

makes admission decisions—i.e., which inpatient unit to admit the patient to—and completes intake formalities. The patient is then transported to the appropriate inpatient unit. For patients who are discharged to their homes, the ED doctor typically provides advise and prescriptions, as needed. ED doctors also prepare patient encounter summaries, which form the basis of billing. A schematic of this workflow is shown in Fig. 10.4.

10.5 Key Management Challenge

Demand for ED services is random. There are times when the demand far exceeds the supply and times when the demand is relatively low. Hospitals hedge and choose a staffing level that balances patient wait times and quality of care. Still, a common consequence of demand variability is overcrowding in EDs. Overcrowding results in:

- Long wait times—dissatisfaction, abandonment
- Ambulance divert (overwhelm) status

Abandonment is measured by counting the number of patients who leave without being seen, which is also referred to as *LWBS*. Hospitals initiate an ambulance divert status when they no longer have ED capacity to take care of additional

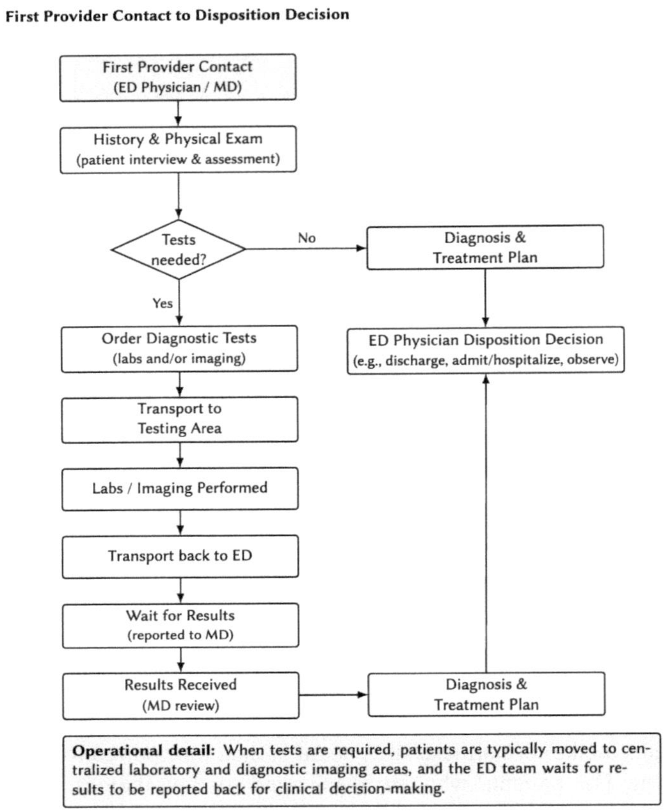

Fig. 10.3 First-provider contact to disposition decision workflow

patients. Ambulances may not bring additional patients to a hospital that has gone on the divert status. However, the hospital is still responsible for walk-in emergency patients, i.e., those that arrive on their own (without being transported in an ambulance). Ambulance diversion is common, although it is costly because the hospital loses potential revenue. Hospitals going on divert status are also bad for patients because they may not be taken to the nearest hospital increasing ambulance travel times and the likelihood of adverse medical outcomes.

Because ED overcrowding is observed in all parts of the USA, it has been the focus of attention of healthcare management scholars. The following reasons have been considered to explain overcrowding:

- Increasing demand trend ⟵ often attributed to EMTALA.
- Variability: Demand, service time, protocols (mix of emergent, urgent and nonurgent patients).
- Boarding: Downstream bed shortages resulting in full ED bed occupancy.

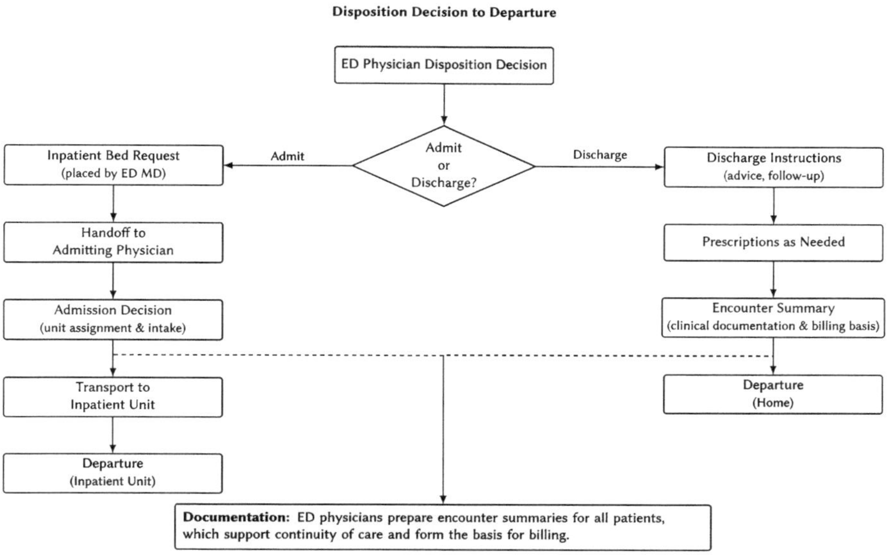

Fig. 10.4 Disposition decision to discharge workflow

From an operations perspective, choosing the *right staffing level* is one of the key challenges for ED managers. This requires modeling-based approaches. However, we begin by considering some common sense approaches first.

Some Common Sense Solutions

- Decrease peak utilization rate. That is, either lower peak arrival rate of the bottleneck resource or increase its service rate during peak periods. Some strategies for achieving both these goals are as follows:
  - Lower peak arrival rate—announce periods when ED is busy, book limited ED appointments.
  - Increase service rate—let non-bottleneck providers do a portion of service (before or after first-provider contact).
- Decrease variability—Simplify and standardize tasks.
- Parallel processing—Order tests while patient is waiting to be seen by MD[1].
- Share the pain—Send boarded patients to other hospital departments.
- Sequence activities—Shortest processing time first rule.
- Exploit psychology of waiting—Get started, provide updates since anxiety makes wait seem longer.

[1] This is controversial. Tests may not be needed (increasing cost), and patients may undergo unnecessary exposure to tests that could cause harm.

How should a hospital manager choose ED staffing levels? This depends on the objective. Several different objectives have been proposed in the literature. Some examples are

- Balking related: LWBS, ambulance diversions
- Time related: Time to MD, ED LOS, or % seen within x hours
- Capacity related: Census approaching or exceeding ED bed capacity, provider surveys

We shall next develop a queueing model of ED. We use this model together with ED LOS and % seen within x hours as primary objectives to determine the ED staffing levels.

10.6 Modeling ED as a Queueing System

Figure 10.5 is a schematic of an ED when viewed as a queueing system. The following notation is utilized in this diagram:

λ = average ED arrival rate (Greek letter lambda), e.g., the number of patients per hour.

μ = average service rate (Greek letter mu), e.g., either ED LOS or the time elapsed from arrival to disposition decision (usually in hours).

$\rho = \lambda/\mu$ = utilization (Greek letter rho).

Throughput rate $= \min\{\lambda, \mu\} = \lambda$, because $\mu \leq \lambda$ is not sustainable.

Recall that two time-related performance criteria that were used for calculating panel sizes are as follows:

- Average wait time must not exceed a threshold that we specify.
- Probability that a patient waits more than x days should be no more than α, where we specify x and α.

To calculate these metrics, we shall use the formulae from queueing theory that we encountered in Chap. 7. For convenience, these formulae are presented in this chapter as well.

$$L \approx \left(\frac{\rho^2(1+C_s^2)}{1+\rho^2 C_s^2}\right)\left(\frac{C_a^2+\rho^2 C_s^2}{2(1-\rho)}\right)+\rho$$

$$W = L/\lambda,$$

Fig. 10.5 ED as a queueing system

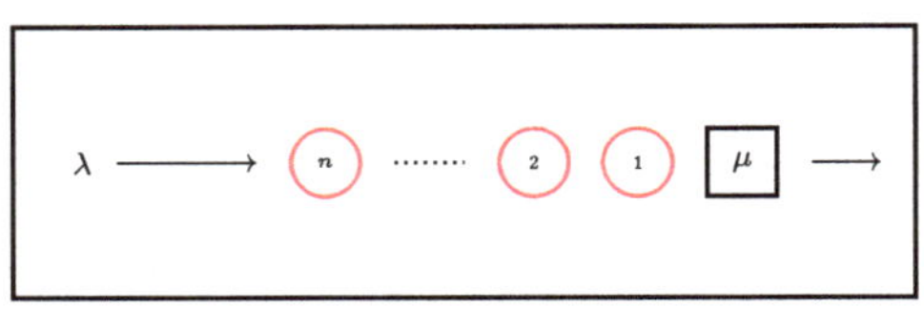

where

$$\begin{aligned}
L &= \text{average number in system} \\
W &= \text{average time in system} \\
C^2 &= \text{scv} = \text{squared coefficient of variation} = \text{variance/(mean)}^2 \\
\rho &= \lambda/\mu = \lambda E[S] = \text{utilization, } E(S) = 1/\mu \\
S &= \text{service time, } E(S) = \text{expected service time.}
\end{aligned}$$

Furthermore, if arrivals are Poisson and service times are exponential, then

$$\text{Prob(Patient time-in-system } \leq x) = 1 - e^{-\mu(1-\rho)x}. \tag{10.1}$$

Therefore, if we want the probability of waiting more than x minutes to not exceed α, then we will set

$$1 - e^{-\mu(1-\rho)x} = 1 - \alpha \Rightarrow \lambda = \mu + \frac{\ln(\alpha)}{x} \Rightarrow \text{minimum } \mu = \lambda - \frac{\ln(\alpha)}{x}. \tag{10.2}$$

This allows us to find the minimum service rate (which can be converted into staffing level) for each x and α. This expression is easy to use and often a good approximation to reality. The application of these concepts is illustrated next with the help of a case study.

10.7 ED Capacity Planning: A Case Study

The ensuing business case is written for the sole purpose of enhancing student learning via classroom discussion. It does not reflect the operations of a real health system. Any resemblance to a real health system is entirely coincidental.

Description The Austin general hospital was experiencing long patient wait times and patients leaving without being seen (LWBS) in its ED. Specifically, the ED Director, herself an emergency room doctor, worried that MD capacity was not enough to handle the volume of ED arrivals.

The ED operated 24 hours a day, 7 days a week. The hospital had 27 private examination rooms and 12 observation rooms. It was also equipped with in-hospital Computed tomography (CT) device for fast imaging and diagnosis. Observation rooms were used to hold patients whose disposition could not be determined by the ED doctors after initial examination. The hospital had work arrangements with 31 board-certified ED physicians who provided care in shifts. ED doctors were the critical resource that determined the ED wait times. Many worked only part-time or occasional shifts. Only eight doctors worked full time for the hospital. The typical MD work shift was 8 hours long. Most nurses worked in three 8-hour shifts: morning (7 a.m. through 3 p.m.), evening (3 p.m. through 11 p.m.), and night (11 p.m. through 7 a.m. next day). Some nurses also worked 12-hour shifts, which covered either the period from 7 a.m. through 7 p.m. or from 7 p.m. to 7 a.m. the next day.

The ED director asked the hospital's IT department for data on recent hourly arrivals to the ED. The IT department came back with data for a period of 11 months. As the director examined this data, she wondered how she might be able to use the data to determine if she needed to hire more ED physicians.

We are provided the same data in a data set named ED_Arrivals.Rda. Using this data set, let us figure out how we may be able to help the ED director improve ED operations. We begin with two visualizations of the arrivals patterns.

10.7.1 Data Visualization

In Fig. 10.6, we plot the raw data pertaining to two separate hours of the day labeled Midnight (from 12 to 1 a.m.) and 3 p.m. (from 3 to 4 p.m.). This same figure was presented in Chap. 9 as Fig. 9.5. The raw data appears to lack a pattern, which makes it difficult to formulate a staffing strategy.

It turns out that a useful way to visualize the same data is by calculating average arrivals in 4-hour intervals aggregated by day of week for each weekday, as shown in Fig. 10.7. This figure also divides the day into six 4-hour intervals and plots average arrival rates within each such interval. Notice that the arrival rate varies within each interval, but that within-interval variability is much smaller than across interval variability. We can utilize this observation to plan for staffing by interval, i.e., on a period-by-period basis. This type of aggregation is often useful in developing a predictive model of MD requirements first, and from there a prescriptive model based on a specified objective and available resources. We illustrate this approach in the remainder of this chapter.

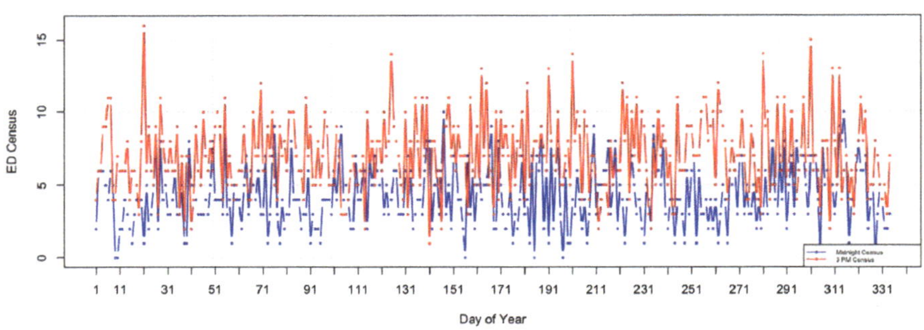

Fig. 10.6 11-month data from a 400-bed community hospital; arrivals 12–1 a.m. and 3–4 p.m.

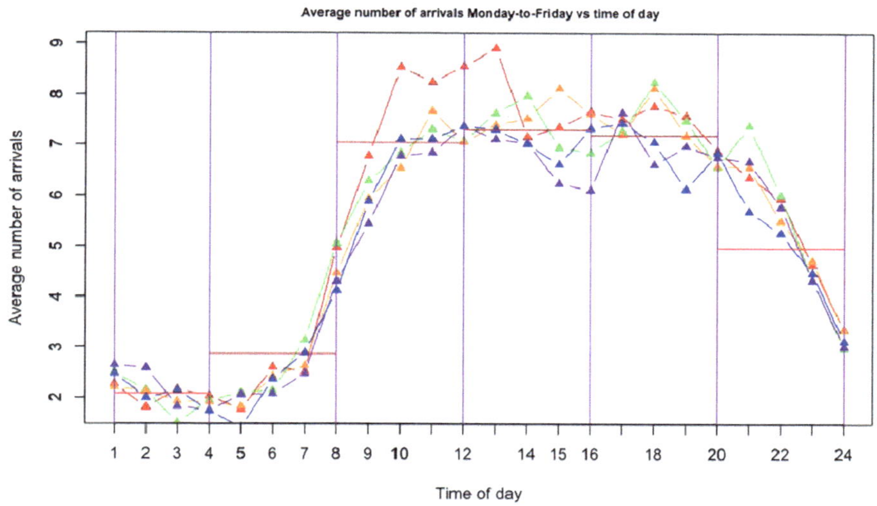

Fig. 10.7 Aggregate ED arrival pattern

10.7.2 Staffing Requirements: Predictive Analytics

- Divide workday into staffing periods.
- Estimate average arrival rate in each staffing period.
- Use the approximate queueing model to calculate minimum staffing level that achieves service target.

This approach is also called SIPP, an acronym for stationary independent period by period. There are two types of inputs for this model: the parameters, i.e., patient arrival rates, and the desired performance targets. We list the performance targets next. The patient arrival rates need to be estimated from the data.

Inputs:

- Time in system performance threshold $= x$.
- Max probability of exceeding the time in system threshold $= \alpha$.
- Example, probability that patients have to spend more than $x = 2$ hours in the ED is no more than $\alpha = 0.2$.

Outputs:

- Staffing requirements for the selected x and α

The Formula

$$\text{Criterion: Prob(Time in System} > x) \leq \alpha.$$

From queueing theory, we obtain

$$\text{Prob(Total Time } \leq x) = 1 - e^{-\mu(1-\rho)x}.$$

Using the fact that $\rho = \lambda/\mu$, the above can be rearranged to obtain

$$\mu = \lambda - \frac{\ln(\alpha)}{x}.$$

- $\mu = n \cdot \mu_0$, where n is the number of MDs, and μ_0 is the mean service rate of each MD.
- Use the above formula to calculate the smallest n that satisfies the above inequality.

An Example Suppose $x = 2$, $\alpha = 0.05$, $\mu_0 = 2$, and $\lambda = 7$.
Because ρ must be less than 1, this means $n > 3.5$

$$n\mu_0 = 7 - \frac{\ln(.05)}{2} = 8.498$$
$$\Rightarrow n = 4.25.$$

We would need to hire five MDs because it is generally not possible to hire a fractional number of MDs. However, if we are allowed to hire MDs in increments of 1/2, then we would hire 4.5 MDs for this time period. Therefore, the answer may depend on the MD work shift constraints.

You will need to repeat this exercise for each 4-hour interval. The numbers you obtain from this exercise are called MD requirements.

10.7.3 Determining Shift Start Times—Prescriptive Analytics

This section requires knowledge of linear programming (see Sect. A.3). It may be skipped without affecting students' understanding of other concepts in this chapter.

How best to allocate a fixed number of MDs to 8-hour shifts to minimize shortage? Recall that MD requirements are different in each 4-hour interval. This problem can be formulated as a linear program and solved using open-source solvers. How?

Let us work this out. Suppose

$$z_{ij} = \begin{cases} 1 \text{ if MD } j \text{ is scheduled to start his/her shift at time } i, \\ 0 \text{ otherwise.} \end{cases}$$

$i \in \{1, 2, \cdots, 6\}$, because there are six 4-hour periods in a day
$j \in \{1, 2, \cdots, m\}$, where m is the number of available MDs.

Let r_i = staffing requirement in period i [from the queueing model]. The ED manager's decision problem is to choose $z_{i,j}$'s. We demonstrate one method that can be used to arrive at a solution.

Because each period is 4 hours, and shifts are 8 hours, ⇒ MDs who begin their shifts in either period $(i-1)$ or period i are available to work in period i.

⇒ # of available MDs in period $i = \sum_{j=1}^{m}[z_{(i-1),j} + z_{i,j}]$, $i > 1$, and no MD can start in period 6.

The ED manager may wish to assign shift start times to minimize total shortage, i.e., select $z_{i,j}$'s such that the sum

$$\{r_1 - \sum_{j=1}^{m} z_{1,j}\}^+ + \sum_{i=2}^{5}\{r_i - \sum_{j=1}^{m}[z_{(i-1),j} + z_{i,j}]\}^+ + \{r_6 - \sum_{j=1}^{m} z_{5,j}\}^+$$

is minimized. The plus sign means the positive part.

We now have a possible objective function. What about constraints?

First Constraint:

$$\sum_{i=1}^{6}\sum_{j=1}^{m} z_{i,j} \le m.$$

This means we cannot assign shift start times to more than m MDs.

Second Constraint:

$$\sum_{i=1}^{6} z_{i,j} \le 1, \quad \text{for every } j = 1, 2, \cdots, m.$$

This means each MD will have at most one shift start time.

Third Constraint:

$$z_{i,j} \in \{0, 1\}.$$

The above formulation is nonlinear! Fortunately, it can be converted into a linear program by defining additional variables that count the number of MDs short in each period.

Let w_i = number of MDs short in period i. Then, $w_i \ge r_i - \sum_{j=1}^{m}[z_{(i-1),j}+z_{i,j}]$, if $i > 1$ and $i < 6$. For the first and the last 4-hour intervals, we have $w_1 \ge r_1 - \sum_{j=1}^{m} z_{1,j}$, and $w_6 \ge r_6 - \sum_{j=1}^{m} z_{5,j}$. Care is needed in the formulation because there are no MDs from the previous 4-hour interval at the start of the day, and no MD is assigned an 8-hour shift starting in the 6th period of the day. We minimize the sum of w_i's, subject to the constraints above, resulting in the following equivalent LP formulation. In this example, the MD requirements are $r_1 = 2$, $r_2 = 2$, $r_3 = 4$, $r_5 = 4$, $r_5 = 4$, and $r_6 = 3$. These are the numbers you see on the right-hand side of constraints 1 through 6 in the formulation below.

$$\min_{z,w} \sum_{i=1}^{6} w_i$$

subject to

$$w_1 + \sum_{j=1}^{m} z_{1j} \geq 2$$

$$w_2 + \sum_{j=1}^{m} z_{2j} + \sum_{j=1}^{m} z_{1j} \geq 2$$

$$w_3 + \sum_{j=1}^{m} z_{3j} + \sum_{j=1}^{m} z_{2j} \geq 4$$

$$w_4 + \sum_{j=1}^{m} z_{4j} + \sum_{j=1}^{m} z_{3j} \geq 4$$

$$w_5 + \sum_{j=1}^{m} z_{5j} + \sum_{j=1}^{m} z_{4j} \geq 4$$

$$w_6 + \sum_{j=1}^{m} z_{5j} \geq 3$$

$$\sum_{i=1}^{5} \sum_{j=1}^{m} z_{ij} \leq m$$

$$\sum_{i=1}^{5} z_{ij} \leq 1, \forall j$$

$$z_{i,j} \in \{0, 1\} \;\; \& \;\; w_i \geq 0.$$

Using LP Solver In order to use a solver, the problem must be next specified in a standard form. Requirements of this specification are as follows:

- Objective function $\longrightarrow$ vector of coefficients
- Constraints $\longrightarrow$ coefficient matrix
- Direction of constraints $\longrightarrow$ direction vector
- RHS values $\longrightarrow$ vector of values

Possible solvers: lpsolve, gurobi, cplex, $\cdots$

Coefficient Matrix with $m = 5$

w1	w2	w3	w4	w5	w6	z11	z21	z31	z41	z51	z12	z22	z32	z42	z52	z13	z23	z33	z43	z53	z14	z24	z34	z44	z54	z15	z25	z35	z45	z55
1	0	0	0	0	0	1	0	0	0	0	1	0	0	0	0	1	0	0	0	0	1	0	0	0	0	1	0	0	0	0
0	1	0	0	0	0	1	1	0	0	0	1	1	0	0	0	1	1	0	0	0	1	1	0	0	0	1	1	0	0	0
0	0	1	0	0	0	0	1	1	0	0	0	1	1	0	0	0	1	1	0	0	0	1	1	0	0	0	1	1	0	0
0	0	0	1	0	0	0	0	1	1	0	0	0	1	1	0	0	0	1	1	0	0	0	1	1	0	0	0	1	1	
0	0	0	0	1	0	0	0	0	1	1	0	0	0	1	1	0	0	0	1	1	0	0	0	1	1	0	0	0	1	1
0	0	0	0	0	1	0	0	0	0	1	0	0	0	0	1	0	0	0	0	1	0	0	0	0	1	0	0	0	0	1
0	0	0	0	0	0	1	1	1	1	1	0	0	0	0	0	0	0	0	0	0	0	0	0	0	0	0	0	0	0	0
0	0	0	0	0	0	0	0	0	0	0	1	1	1	1	1	0	0	0	0	0	0	0	0	0	0	0	0	0	0	0
0	0	0	0	0	0	0	0	0	0	0	0	0	0	0	0	1	1	1	1	1	0	0	0	0	0	0	0	0	0	0
0	0	0	0	0	0	0	0	0	0	0	0	0	0	0	0	0	0	0	0	0	1	1	1	1	1	0	0	0	0	0
0	0	0	0	0	0	0	0	0	0	0	0	0	0	0	0	0	0	0	0	0	0	0	0	0	0	1	1	1	1	1
0	0	0	0	0	0	1	1	1	1	1	1	1	1	1	1	1	1	1	1	1	1	1	1	1	1	1	1	1	1	1

Solution with $m = 5$

Total number of half shifts short = 9. Our solution, though not unique, does not waste any MD capacity because we have 10 available 1/2 shifts, whereas the daily staffing requirements add up to 19 half shifts.

Shortages:

$$w_1^* = 1$$
$$w_2^* = 1$$
$$w_3^* = 3$$
$$w_4^* = 2$$
$$w_5^* = 1$$
$$w_6^* = 1$$

Assignments:

$$z_{5,1}^* = 1$$
$$z_{4,2}^* = 1$$
$$z_{5,3}^* = 1$$
$$z_{3,4}^* = 1$$
$$z_{1,5}^* = 1$$

Note that the optimal assignment is not unique. There are other assignments that will result in the same amount of total shortage. Therefore, you may want the solution to avoid large shortages in any 4-hour interval. These types of considerations result in the need to perform sensitivity analysis. Some variations you may try to work out are as follows:

- Different number of MDs
- Different cost coefficients for different periods
- Different shift lengths, e.g., 4, 8, and 12 hours
- Fairness—equalizing workload per MD in each period

Chapter 11
Managing Operating Rooms

11.1 OR Patient Flow

A variety of resources are needed at each step of the patient flow through the surgical suites. Registration area is typically staffed by administrative personnel. Pre-op area processes require anesthesiologists, nurses, and health technicians. Operating rooms require a whole host of resources including surgeons, anesthesiologists, surgical packs, nurses, and health technicians. PACU stands for postanesthesia care unit, ICU stands for intensive care unit, and inpatient unit refers to areas with staffed hospital beds where patients recover or receive further treatment. Some patients leave after recovering in a PACU, and others require longer recovery period, which typically occurs in an appropriate inpatient unit. Some patients need to be taken to the ICU immediately after surgery for recovery and further treatment. Operating rooms need to be cleaned and made ready for the next procedure after the completion of each surgery. This is referred to as *turnover*. The amount of time needed for turnover is typically 15–30 minutes (A patient flow diagram is shown in Fig. 11.1).

11.2 OR Managers' Challenges

Big Picture: Staffed ORs are costly, but surgical services are also a significant source of revenue for most hospitals. Still, OR utilization in the USA is relatively low, which begs the question following questions: "why is OR utilization low in US hospitals?" and "what can OR managers do to improve efficiency of OR processes while maintaining desired patient outcomes?" We shall examine some of these levers in this chapter. The OR managers' challenges can be categorized by time scale, as described in several remarks next.

D. Gupta, *Healthcare Analytics*, Springer Texts in Business and Economics,
https://doi.org/10.1007/978-3-032-24835-0_11

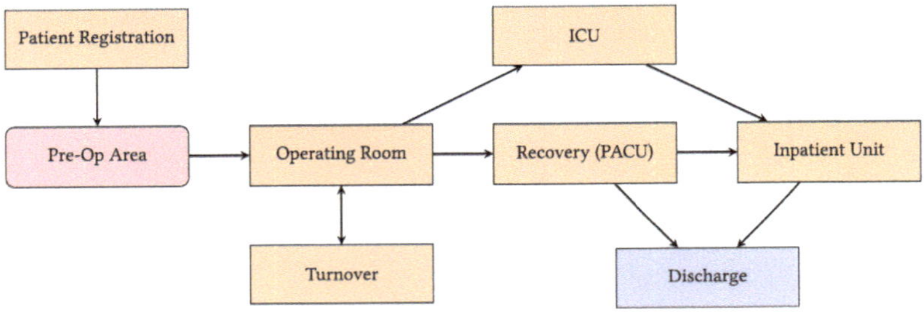

Fig. 11.1 OR patient flow

Exhibit 6: Long-term challenges

- Staffed ORs cost on average $\approx$ $15 per minute
- Yet, OR utilization is low in the US ($\sim 50\%$)
- How many ORs should a hospital have?
- What can OR managers do to improve utilization (lower cost) without adversely affecting outcomes?

Most US hospitals assign guaranteed blocks of time either to surgical services or to individual surgeons in advance. Many block surgeons do not fully utilize assigned OR capacity. Some surgical services have less than 100% utilization of their assigned capacity, and at the same time significant usage of overtime. Some hospitals have dedicated ORs for urgent cases. These practices give rise to the medium-term challenges listed in the highlighted remark below.

Exhibit 7: Medium-term Challenges

- How much OR capacity to allocate to each service or surgeon?
- Should the hospital have one or more ORs dedicated for urgent / emergent cases?
- How to staff ORs? – how many anesthesiologists, nurses, and health techs to hire?
- How many copies of each type of OR equipment to purchase?

A whole host of challenges also exist in the short term. In fact, one could argue that the short-term decisions have a significant effect on operating costs, and patient and surgeon satisfaction. They are also more amenable to mathematical modeling and data-driven decision-making. Models presented in this chapter pertain mostly to short-term challenges. A list of short-term challenges is provided in the highlighted remark below.

Exhibit 8: Short-term Challenges

- Which surgeries to schedule in which ORs?
- In what sequence should surgeries be scheduled?
- How to accommodate surgeon preferences (DoW, ToD, Support staff)
- How much capacity to reserve for urgent/ emergent cases?
- What protocols to use to deal with disruptions, e.g., surgeries running late, patient no shows, etc.

OR managers need to decide which surgeries to schedule in which ORs, unless block assignments also include specific OR allocations. In many cases, surgeons determine the surgery sequence in their dedicated blocks. In some other cases, surgeries are scheduled by a central scheduler. A common approach involves a mix of surgeon-driven and central scheduler-driven scheduling and sequencing of cases. After cases are scheduled, it is common to have urgent and add-on cases added to existing OR schedule, resulting in overtime. Finally, there may be planned or unplanned disruptions to the schedule, which introduce many more management challenges.

In addition to operational factors, a variety of other factors influence OR utilization. We list some of those next:

- Surgical specialty/surgeon rather than asset-focused approach—because hospitals want to attract the best surgeons
- Incentive misalignment—separate payment to hospitals and physicians with the result that physicians may not care about hospital efficiency
- Competition for top surgeons—this leads to hospitals using guaranteed access to OR time as a bargaining chip with surgeons

We shall devote the remainder of this chapter on understanding the impact of sequential booking practice.

Note that sequential booking may exist in both block and non-block scheduling practices! We shall next examine pros and cons of block booking.

Block Booking—*pros and cons*

The Pros:

- Allows hospital to attract top surgeons.
- Allows surgeons to divide their time into clinic time and OR time.
- Allows surgeons to promise surgery dates to patients during outpatient visits.

The Cons:

- Loss of control over case booking.
- Often results in low utilization of staffed OR time.
- Ensuring availability of equipment and support staff may be harder.

11.3 Surgical Case Scheduling

Let us consider an example. Surgical case booking requests with case lengths d_1, $d_2, \cdots$ arrive one at a time. Decisions must be made immediately. The scheduler uses a first-come first-served (fair) policy and books the first three cases as follows:

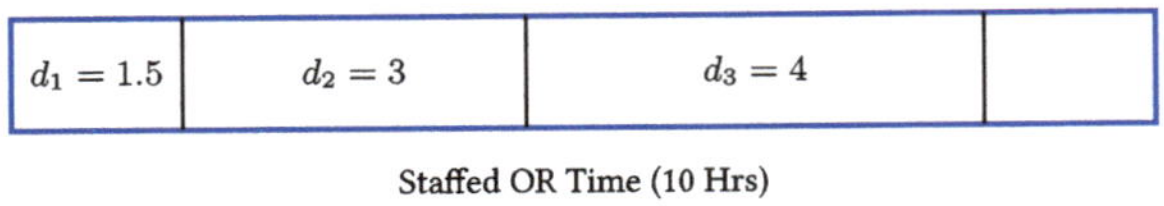

Suppose $d_4 = 2$, $d_5 = 5$, $d_6 = 3$, and no other case booking requests arrive for this OR block. Clearly, cases 4 through 6 do not fit in the available staffed OR time. The following questions then naturally arise:

- What is the OR utilization?
- Answer: Utilization $= \frac{8.5}{10} = 0.85$.
- What causes the utilization to be low?
- Answer: Perhaps the fact that the scheduler does not observe all of the cases that need to be scheduled for that day.
- What if the scheduler waited to observe the entire case sequence before scheduling any cases? How does that affect scheduling?
- Answer: The answer will depend on the algorithm that the scheduler uses. For example, suppose the scheduler acted greedily. Then:
  - d_5 will be scheduled first. d_3 will be scheduled next.
  - Utilization will be $= 9/10 = 0.9$.
  - This is not bad.
- But, we wonder if there a better way?
- Answer: Yes, there is a better way!
  - Consider scheduling d_2, d_3, and d_6.
  - Now, the utilization $= 10/10 = 1$!
  - This is an optimal solution because utilization cannot exceed 1. However, it is not unique. There are other combinations of surgical cases that result in a utilization of 1.

How can we consistently find an optimal (or near-optimal) mix of cases? It appears that being able to observe the entire case sequence increases scheduling flexibility and results in a more efficient solution. But, is that practical? How can a hospital implement the strategy that relies on observing case sequence in practice? We tackle these issues next.

11.3.1 Case Booking and Scheduling Optimization

Suppose, we are given the following data:

ℓ = shift (or block) length.
$L = \{1, \cdots, m\}$ = a known sequence of m cases.
d_j = length of the j-th case.

Our decision variables are

$$x_j = \begin{cases} 1 \text{ if case } j \text{ is selected,} \\ 0 \text{ otherwise,} \end{cases}$$

for every $j = 1, 2, \cdots, n$, where m is the number of cases.
If we have this data, we can formulate a mathematical optimization problem to find the optimal selection of cases to schedule. This formulation is presented next.

$$\max_{\{x_1,\cdots,x_m\}} \sum_{j=1}^{m} x_j d_j$$

Subject to:

$$\sum_{j=1}^{m} x_j d_j \leq \ell$$

$$x_j \in \{0, 1\}.$$

In the above expression, the symbol $\sum_{j=1}^{m}$ means summation over the index j from 1 through m. Upon solving the above optimization problem, we will obtain an optimal selection of cases that will maximize the total amount of OR time utilized.

In practice, OR managers can realize benefits similar to those of observing the entire case sequence by utilizing a two-step approach in which they first accept a certain number of cases for a particular future day, based on aggregate capacity, and then schedule. While this approach can lead to improved utilization, it can also lead to situations in which all accepted cases cannot be scheduled without incurring some overtime. Let us see how this may work out via an example.

A hospital first decides which surgical cases to accept for a future day. Then, one day before surgeries are to take place, and the hospital places all accepted cases into ORs to achieve the minimum total staffing cost. The cost of opening an OR during regular working hours is c_R per minute, and the overtime cost is c_O per minute. Assume that $c_O > c_R$. The regular working hours are from 7 a.m. to 3 p.m., i.e., a single 8-hour shift. Suppose on a particular day, the hospital has chosen to open m ORs using regular staff. The realized case lengths (in minutes) are $d_1, d_2 \cdots, d_n$. Note that this means that n cases have been accepted and must

be scheduled. How will we formulate the hospital's problem of choosing an optimal allocation of surgical cases to ORs for this day?
Solution: We will first define the following decision variables:

$$x_{ij} = \begin{cases} 1 \text{ if surgery } i \text{ is assigned to OR } j, \\ 0 \text{ otherwise.} \end{cases}$$

$$O_j = \text{the amount of overtime used by OR } j.$$

Next, we will write our objective function and necessary constraints. One may think of the objective as being that of minimizing total staffing cost, including overtime. However, the cost of opening m ORs using regular staff is sunk. Therefore, it does not appear in the objective function listed next.

$$\min_{\{x_{ij}, O_j\}} c_O \sum_{j=1}^{m} O_j.$$

The constraints are as follows:

$$\text{Constraint 1: } \sum_{j=1}^{m} x_{ij} = 1 \qquad \text{for every } i$$

$$\text{Constraint 2: } \sum_{i=1}^{n} x_{ij} d_i \leq 480 + O_j \qquad \text{for every } j$$

$$\text{Constraint 3: } x_{ij} \in \{0, 1\}$$

$$\text{Constraint 4: } O_j \geq 0.$$

These constraints can be explained as follows. The first constraint ensures that each case i is scheduled in exactly one OR—because x_{ij} are either 0 or 1 (from Constraint 3), upon requiring their sum to be 1 over all j, we effectively require that exactly one OR is assigned to each surgery i. Note that there are m such constraints. Next, the second constraint keeps track of the amount of time needed for surgeries scheduled in each OR. In the left-hand side of this constraint, we sum $x_{ij}d_i$ over all i, for each fixed j, to find the total amount of time needed to complete surgeries assigned to OR j. On the right-hand side, we have available minutes. There are 8 hours in regular time, yielding 480 minutes, and O_j minutes in overtime. The second constraint thus says that the demand for OR minutes from OR j must be no more than the supply. The third and the fourth constraints restrict possible values of x_{ij} and O_j. Note that because our objective is to minimize overtime, Constraint 2 will be tight if $O_j > 0$, which means its LHS will equal the RHS in such cases. Formulations such as this and others we have encountered before can be solved using standard optimization software, such as `lpsolve` in R.

Challenges: The approach we have outlined is a stylized model. Real-life examples are much more complex and require additional effort. For example, we may be faced with the following challenges:

- Does this scale to multiple ORs? ✓
- How do we leverage data? ✓
- Estimates of d_js are almost always wrong!

The items that are indicated with a check mark can be overcome with some effort. However, having random d_js makes this a very hard problem. In that case, either underutilization or over time is inevitable!

In Part IV of this book, you will find two short cases that focus on pre-op and OR scheduling challenges. These cases are designed to highlight OR management challenges in real settings as well as provide representative data that can be used to illustrate concepts discussed in earlier parts of this chapter.

Chapter 12
Managing Inpatient Units

12.1 Introduction

Inpatient units are often a significant portion of the physical facilities of a hospital. Managing their operations is both complex and challenging. A whole host of issues arise ranging from the design of the units to protocols for handling nurse shortages within shifts. This book does not intend to provide a comprehensive survey of all such issues, focusing instead on two issues that fall within the purview of operations managers. These are (1) degree of specialization and (2) aggregate staffing.

Most hospitals create different patient care units for different diagnoses, e.g., neurosurgery, orthopedics, and urology units dedicated to surgical patients by the type of service. In addition, there are units organized by the intensity of care needed, e.g., intensive care units (ICUs) and step-down units. Finally, there may be units dedicated to child birth, cancer treatment, and behavioral health. Specialization serves to improve quality of care. Nurses become more efficient and effective at caring for certain types of patients. Nurses generally prefer to work in specialized inpatient units. Patient satisfaction is also higher when they are placed in specialized units. However, from an efficiency viewpoint, specialization can lead to unequal utilization of beds in different units in the short term, with overcrowding in some units and empty beds in others. Caring for patients with different diagnoses in the same unit overcomes this shortcoming, but it requires cross-training of nurses and may result in lower nurse satisfaction and lower efficiency and effectiveness of care. General purpose units may experience greater nurse turnover and lower patient satisfaction. Regardless of the choice of specialization, nurses are typically assigned to a particular unit, which is referred to as their home unit.

Staffing inpatient units presents its own unique challenges. Nurses' salaries are typically considered fixed costs because the number of nurses on staff cannot be varied at a short notice. Note that there is also a shortage of nurses, which makes it difficult to attract nurses without offering them favorable terms. Nurses work in shifts, which are typically 8, 10, or 12 hours long. If nurses work full time, and

D. Gupta, *Healthcare Analytics*, Springer Texts in Business and Economics,
https://doi.org/10.1007/978-3-032-24835-0_12

shifts are 8 hours long, then they will be available for five shifts in a week. However, patient care is provided 24 hours a day, 7 days a week. This means that in addition to deciding how many nurses to hire for each shift, a unit manager must also decide which nurses will work in which shifts.

For the purpose of our discussion, we shall assume 8-hour nurse shifts and refer to them as day (D), evening (E), and night (N) shifts. Typically, day shifts are from 7 a.m. to 3 p.m., evening shifts are from 3 p.m. to 11 p.m., and night shifts are from 11 p.m. to 7 a.m. the next day. There are rules or negotiated contracts with nurses' unions (collective bargaining units), governing how many different shift types a nurse may be asked to work in during each 2-week (pay) period. For example, the nurse manager may be restricted to switching shift assignments at most twice during each pay period for a particular nurse. In addition to D, E, and N shift types, an additional variation comes from weekend versus weekday shifts. Nurses, like most of us, prefer to have their weekends off. To come up with an equitable solution, often nurse assignments are such that a nurse may be asked to work no more than 1 weekend in each 2-week period. This introduces additional constraints on nurse staffing.

Drilling deeper into the operations of an inpatient unit within a shift, the HUC has to decide which nurses will take care of which patients. Such assignments attempt to balance nurses' seniority, expertise, continuity of care, and workload. In fact, many states have enacted rules that limit how many patients may be assigned to a nurse in a single shift. The latter are referred to as *nurse-to-patient (N:P) ratios*. These decisions are further complicated by planned and unplanned time off. Planned time off is typically requested several weeks in advance. However, unplanned absences may be caused by a whole host of unforeseen events such as illness, weather, family emergency, and childcare needs. Target N:P ratios are specific to each inpatient unit and each shift. Target N:P ratios may change across D, E, and N shifts and across weekday and weekend shifts. However, they do not change for each fixed shift type, as characterized by day of week and shift type. In contrast, the actual N:P ratios can and do vary across shifts of the same type depending on the availability of nurses and patient census.

12.2 Management Strategies

It should be clear from the above discussion that a major challenge for hospital managers is the balancing of demand and supply of nursing care. The inpatient volume (also referred to as "census"), the intensity of care needs (also referred to as patient "acuity"), and lengths of stay are random. However, they are not completely unpredictable. In fact, historical census and acuity data could be used to predict nursing requirements, albeit such predictions are noisy. Upon knowing nurse requirements, models developed in earlier chapters in this book, in particular, the newsvendor model, can be utilized to determine an appropriate hedging strategy for determining the long-term nurse staffing levels. While these strategies may be optimized in the aggregate to determine the number of nurses to have on the hospital's payroll, there is invariably a mismatch between realized availability of nurses and demand for nursing care in a shift. Such mismatches require that top-level nurse managers develop strategies for dealing with short-term mismatches.

Broadly speaking, the short-term strategies available to hospital managers can be classified into two groups: proactive and reactive. A careful coordination across these two types of strategies is necessary because neither is sufficient by itself. The remainder of this section discusses several examples in each category.

Pro-active Strategies

1. *Float nurses*/ pools: Depending on the nurses' expertise and terms of employment contracts, it may be possible to "float" some nurses from one unit to another to realize a better balance between availability of nursing care and patient requirements. Nurses that agree to float are sometimes called float nurses. Some hospitals go a step further and create a pool of nurses who do not have a home unit, but have agreed to work in one of several units depending on the need. These nurses are assigned to a unit only at the start of their shifts. This strategy is meant to overcome workload imbalances caused by nurses' planned and unplanned time off.
2. *Delayed bed assignment*: When hospitals specialize inpatient units, they also develop patient placement guidelines. The guidelines may specify primary, secondary, and tertiary patient diagnoses (diagnosis-related group (DRG) codes) for which each unit's nurses are capable of providing patient care. Thus, it would be possible to place a patient in one of several units although the preferred placement would be to a unit whose set of primary diagnoses includes the patient's reason for admission to the hospital. The latter is referred to as the "admit code."

   Many hospitals assign a bed to a patient at the time of arrival to the hospital, e.g., when they arrive at the hospital to undergo a surgery. Bed availability is fluid and changes throughout the day because of new admissions, discharges, and transfers across inpatient units. In many such cases, it helps to delay bed assignment until such time that the patient is ready to be transported to the inpatient unit. Delayed assignments can take advantage of the most up to date information when making bed assignment decisions and result in virtual pooling of inpatient beds. This strategy works particularly well when different inpatient units are specialized for specific primary diagnoses, but possess overlapping capabilities in terms of secondary diagnoses. It is not necessary for every unit to have a large number of secondary and tertiary diagnoses so long as the capabilities of different units overlap, creating a chain. Limited flexibility of this sort has been found to be an effective strategy in the context of manufacturing systems as well.
3. *On-call nurses*: A typical hospital employs hundreds of nurses. Many work part time and many are willing to work extra shifts to increase their earnings. This provides an opportunity for hospital managers. In some cases, they offer incentives for nurses to sign up to be on call. The incentive is in the form of

extra pay, regardless of whether they are asked to do extra shifts or not. In return, nurses agree to pick up a certain number of extra shifts in each pay period, e.g., up to 2 extra shifts in a 2-week period. The nurses are also paid an additional amount for each extra shift. This strategy incurs an up-front cost, but avoids the need to hire temporary or agency nurses in a reactive mode.

Reactive Strategies

1. *Temporary/agency nurses*: There are instances when proactive strategies are not adequate to meet patient care requirements. In such cases, hospitals utilize the services of agencies that supply temporary nurses on an on-demand basis. Temporary nurses cost more and are typically neither as efficient nor as effective as the salaried nurses because they are not as familiar with the work environment. For this reason, hospitals utilize temporary nurses only as a last resort.
2. *Patient transfers*: Some inpatient units are in high demand relative to supply. For example, with N:P ratio of 1:1, ICU beds are an expensive resource. Therefore, hospitals keep the number of ICU beds low and their utilization high. On occasions when bed demand exceeds capacity, which is not uncommon, hospitals sometimes transfer certain patients from ICU to step-down units. This frees up capacity in the ICU. However, it consumes nurses' time and could result in longer length of stay (LOS). Similar patient transfers can occur across other units, e.g., from step down units to general wards and vice versa.[1]
3. *Swing units*: Some hospitals use swing units that open and close as needed in response to census fluctuations. This strategy can help hospitals maintain uniform core staffing in primary units, but hospitals need extra nurses that can be hired on a temporary basis to staff swing units. Therefore, such a strategy may not be practical when nurses are in short supply.

12.3 Delayed Bed Assignment Strategy

In this section, we quantify the impact of delayed bed assignment, which results in virtual pooling, with the help of an example. The data used in this example are not real.

A hospital has two identical inpatient units with nursing requirements (which we call demand) D_1 and D_2. Suppose D_1 and D_2 are normally distributed with mean

[1] Patient transfers necessitated by lack of capacity should not be confused with transfers necessitated by clinical factors. For example, there are instances when changes to patients' clinical diagnoses require greater intensity of care, and patients are transferred from general wards to step-down units, or from step-down units to ICUs. To avoid such transfers, some hospitals have invested in acuity-adaptable (universal) beds that patients can occupy during their entire hospital stay. Under this strategy, patients are not transferred from one unit to another, but the N:P ratio is adjusted to match the acuity level of each patient during their sojourn. Acuity-adaptable beds cost more and require frequent adjustments to the level of nursing care provided. Specifically, N:P ratios in such units vary across patients and across time.

$\mu_1 = 7$ and $\mu_2 = 8$ and standard deviations $\sigma_1 = 2$ and $\sigma_2 = 2.25$. The hospital determines staffing levels of the two units independently to achieve a critical ratio of 0.75 (ratio of c_u to $c_u + c_o$). Given this data, how would we calculate the staffing requirements, rounded to the next highest 0.25 shift, in these two units?

Answer

We use the Newsvendor model to arrive at the following answer upon using the qnorm function in R:

Unit #	Demand	CR	Optimal requirements
1	$N(\mu_1 = 7, \sigma_1 = 2)$	0.75	= qnorm(0.75, 7, 2, lower.tail = TRUE) = 8.35
2	$N(\mu_1 = 8, \sigma_1 = 2.25)$	0.75	= qnorm(0.75, 8, 2.25, lower.tail = TRUE) = 9.52.

Upon rounding to the next higher 0.25, we get 8.5 and 9.75 nurses, for a total of 18.25 nurses.

Next, let us calculate the probability that a patient who needs to be placed in unit 1 will be boarded, and repeat the calculations for unit 2. We obtain the following result upon using the cumulative distribution function (CDF) of the normal distribution.

Unit #	Prob of boarding
1	$P(D_1 > 8.5) =$ pnorm(8.5, mean = 7, sd = 2, lower.tail = FALSE) = 0.227
2	$P(D_2 > 9.75) =$ pnorm(9.75, mean = 8, sd = 2.25, lower.tail = FALSE) = 0.218.

Next, suppose the demand patterns in the two units are independent of each other, and the hospital management decides to pool nursing capacity by utilizing the delayed bed assignment strategy. What is the optimal number of nurses that should be hired? What is the probability that a patient who needs to be placed in either unit 1 or unit 2 will be boarded?

Answer

First, we note that D_{1+2} is also normally distributed with mean $\mu_{1+2} = 7+8 = 15$, and standard deviation $\sigma_{1+2} = \sqrt{\sigma_1^2 + \sigma_2^2} = 3.01$. The calculations of mean and standard deviation of D_{1+2} are valid for any distribution of nurse requirements. However, the observation that D_{1+2} has a normal distribution is true only when D_1 and D_2 have a normal distribution. Therefore, the optimal number of nurses required = qnorm(0.75, 15, 3.01, lower.tail = TRUE) = 17.03, which will be rounded to 17.25. Next, we find the probability of patient boarding as follows:

$$= P(D_{1+2} > 17.25)$$

$$= \text{pnorm}(17.25, \text{mean} = 15, \text{sd} = 3.01, \text{lower.tail} = \text{FALSE})$$

$$= 0.23.$$

This example shows that virtual pooling lowers cost. Why does that happen? There are multiple ways to explain this observation. Here is one such explanation.

Overage and underage costs are sensitive to the value of SCV. Higher the SCV, the higher these costs would be, especially when the random quantity is normally distributed. Prior to pooling, the squared coefficient of variation (SCV) values for demand were as follows:

- Unit 1 SCV of demand = $\frac{2^2}{7^2} = 0.08163$.
- Unit 2 SCV of demand = $\frac{2.25^2}{8^2} = 0.07910$.
- After pooling, the pooled demand's SCV = $\frac{3.01^2}{15^2} = 0.04027$, which is smaller than the SCV of either unit's demand prior to pooling.

Chapter 13
Exercises for Part III

13.1 Discussion Questions

- Develop a hierarchy of emergency department (ED) management challenges by grouping the issues discussed in Chap. 10 into long-, medium-, and short-term categories.
- Upon analyzing hospital data, it is not uncommon to find that the intraday demand for inpatient beds from ED is not more variable than a similar demand from surgical procedures. Discuss why this could happen and its consequences.
- Discuss the pros and cons of block booking. Why do you think block booking is more prevalent in the United States than other countries?
- Discuss the pros and cons of specializing inpatient units.
- Suppose we draw a parallel between hospital patient flow and the flow of raw materials through a factory. In this thought experiment, the work-in-progress inventory in a hospital will be the backlog of patients waiting for the next treatment or intervention, e.g., patients who have been admitted to a hospital and are waiting for certain diagnostic tests to be completed before the next phase of their treatment can begin. Compare and contrast the consequences of such backlog in a hospital setting to that in a factory setting. What are the implications for hospital managers?

13.2 Multiple-Choice Questions

1. Which of the following statements helps explain why hospitals pool demand across multiple inpatient units? Select the single best choice.

   - Pooling lowers overall staffing costs.
   - Pooling decreases nurse-to-patient ratio.

D. Gupta, *Healthcare Analytics*, Springer Texts in Business and Economics,
https://doi.org/10.1007/978-3-032-24835-0_13

- Demand pooling improves nurses' morale.
- Nurses' unions often require that hospitals use demand pooling.
- Demand pooling increases patient satisfaction.

2. Why do many US hospitals offer guaranteed blocks of operating room (OR) time to surgeons? Select the single best answer.

   - To improve OR utilization
   - To attract top surgeons
   - To reduce patient waiting time
   - To streamline OR scheduling
   - To reduce surgery cancellations

3. Which of the following strategies could help a hospital reduce ED congestion during peak demand periods without violating any laws and regulations? Select the single best answer.

   - Hire a greeter to welcome patients to the ED.
   - Require patients to preregister before coming to the ED.
   - Simplify and standardize tasks performed by nurses and health technicians.
   - Incentivize physicians to discharge patients quickly during peak demand periods.
   - Reduce the size of the ED waiting area and prevent patients from entering the ED when waiting area fills up.

4. A profit maximizing hospital has only one OR and five surgeons who compete for access to OR time. The hospital asks each surgeon to submit their surgery scheduling requests for a future date at least one week in advance. Once all requests are known, the hospital uses historical data for each type of surgery to determine the amount of OR time needed for that surgery. It also calculates its net profit from each surgery and then schedules as many surgeries as it can in the OR to maximize its total profit. The OR operates for 10 hours each weekday. No surgeries are performed during weekends. The hospital does not have an ED and does not perform nonscheduled surgeries. There are a total of ten types of procedures performed by the five surgeons.

   Suppose surgeon i submits requests to schedule d_{ij} surgeries of type j for a future date. Note that d_{ij} is non-negative and integer valued. The hospital assesses OR time requirements (in minutes) to be $t_{i,j}$ for surgery j if performed by the i-th surgeon. Note that surgery times may be different for different surgeons even for the same surgery type. It also calculates that each type j surgery will generate a net profit of r_j. Let x_{ij} denote the number of type j surgeries of physician i scheduled by the hospital. Note that $x_{i,j} \geq 0$ and integer valued. Given this setup, which of the following choices is a valid objective function for the hospital? Select the single best answer.

   - $\max\{\sum_{j=1}^{10} r_j x_{i,j}\}$
   - $\max\{\sum_{j=1}^{10} r_j \sum_{i=1}^{5} d_{i,j}\}$

- $\max\{\sum_{i=1}^{5}\sum_{j=1}^{10} x_{i,j}\}$
- $\max\{\sum_{i=1}^{5}\sum_{j=1}^{10} d_{i,j}\}$
- $\max\{\sum_{i=1}^{5}\sum_{j=1}^{10} r_j x_{i,j}\}$

5. In the problem stated above, which of the following is a valid OR availability constraint? Select the single best answer.

- $\sum_{i=1}^{5}\sum_{j=1}^{10} t_{i,j}x_{i,j} \leq 600$
- $\sum_{j=1}^{10} t_{i,j}d_{i,j} \leq 600$
- $\sum_{i=1}^{5}\sum_{j=1}^{10} r_j t_{i,j}x_{i,j} \leq 600$
- $\sum_{i=1}^{5}\sum_{j=1}^{10} d_{i,j}t_{i,j} \leq 600$
- $\sum_{i=1}^{5}\sum_{j=1}^{10} t_{i,j} \leq 600$

13.3 Long-Answer Questions

Problem 13.1 A hospital has two identical inpatient units with nursing requirements (which we call demand) D_1 and D_2. Suppose D_1 and D_2 are normally distributed with mean $\mu_1 = 10$ and $\mu_2 = 12$ and standard deviations $\sigma_1 = 3$ and $\sigma_2 = 3.25$. The hospital determines staffing levels of the two units independently to achieve a critical ratio of 0.8 (ratio of c_u to $c_u + c_o$).

1. Calculate the staffing requirements, rounded to the next highest 0.25 shift, in these two units.
2. Suppose the demand patterns in the two units are correlated with a correlation coefficient $R = 0.4$. If the two units decide to pool nursing capacity and hire an optimal number of nurses after pooling, what would be the optimal number of nurses required?

Hint: $\text{Var}(D_1 + D_2) = \sigma_1^2 + \sigma_2^2 + 2R\sigma_1\sigma_2$.

Note: If your calculator does not allow you to calculate normal quantiles and probabilities, you may write your answers in terms of *qnorm* and *pnorm* functions in R.

Problem 13.2 An ED manager is trying to determine how to assign medical doctors (MDs) currently on the hospital's payroll to meet MD requirements in the ED for each shift and each day of week. There are n available MDs and the ED operates 24 hours a day, 7 days a week. Work shifts are 8-hour long beginning at 7 a.m., 3 p.m., and 11 p.m. An MD can be assigned to at most one shift on any day of week (dow) and to a total of 5 shifts in a week. The ED manager has calculated that on average, the ED needs r_{jk} MDs to be on duty on dow j in shift k. The ED manager wants to make sure that the allocation of MDs to shifts is fair. She asks for your help. Upon inquiring what she means by "fair," she responds that it means no single day of week and shift should have large shortages. You ask if it would be appropriate to minimize the maximum number of MDs short in any shift, and she agrees. You decide to formulate the ED manager's MD shift assignment problem as a linear program.

1. Provide full details of how you would do so.
2. How will you modify the formulation if an MD may not be assigned to different shift start times during the week?

Part IV
Short Cases

Chapter 14
Eagle Health, Inc. (A)

The ensuing business case is written for the sole purpose of enhancing student learning via classroom discussion. It does not reflect the operations of a real health system. Any resemblance to a real health system is entirely coincidental.

Snow had fallen early in the morning, which made traffic slower than usual. John Corleone, JC to his work colleagues, was dreading being late for an important meeting with Nancy Whitaker, MD, the chief medical office (CMO) of Eagle Health, Inc. He was more worried than usual because he did not have answers to questions that Dr. Whitaker had asked him a week ago. Just as he was formulating his response by talking aloud while driving, a car several vehicles ahead of him skidded on an icy patch making it necessary for him to change lanes to avoid collision. He was lucky that he was not involved in a collision although a couple of cars ahead of him were rear-ended. The near miss shook JC, and he forced himself to concentrate only on driving until he reached his office.

Eagle Health, Inc. is named after Eagle Mountain, the highest natural point in Minnesota at 2301 feet. It is located in the Boundary Waters Canoe Area Wilderness and Superior National Forest in the Misquah Hills, northwest of Grand Marais. Eagle Health is a large integrated health services provider that runs 70+ outpatient clinics and more than a dozen hospitals in several upper Midwest states. It is headquartered in Minneapolis, MN. With a total bed capacity exceeding 3000 beds, and several thousand medical doctors (MDs) in full- and part-time work arrangements, it is the one of the largest providers of medical services in the states where it operates. Eagle Health is a well-managed organization that has won several regional and national service-quality awards.

JC was hired as a senior healthcare analyst right after completing his MBA about 2 years ago. Before completing his MBA, he had a couple of years of experience working as an assistant clinic manager. His was a new position created by Eagle to leverage data to improve healthcare operations. JC was hired as Eagle struggled to install a system-wide electronic medical record (EMR) system at enormous cost. In fact, JC's primary assignment was to smooth out kinks in the EMR installation. JC

D. Gupta, *Healthcare Analytics*, Springer Texts in Business and Economics,
https://doi.org/10.1007/978-3-032-24835-0_14

reported directly to the CMO. He was the chief of the fledgling Health Improvement and Analytics department. So far, that department had only one other employee—Jason Lee, a recent data science graduate with expertise in statistics and computer science.

At about the same time that the EMR system went live about a year ago, Eagle implemented the same-day appointment scheduling in some of its clinics as part of its efforts to implement advanced access paradigm for managing clinic capacity—see Murray and Berwick (2003) and Gupta et al. (2006). The idea behind this approach was to reduce backlog to the point that patients who called for an appointment could get an appointment on the same day they called (interpreted as within 24 hours of the time when they called). There were clearly several benefits of this approach. It allowed patients to have quick access to MDs and other service providers and potentially reduced cancellations that were believed to be associated with long appointment delays. However, several senior MDs from the clinics that had implemented the same-day paradigm had complained that the new arrangement was leading to worse continuity of care (CoC) and increased spoilage of appointment slots.

As JC's car turned into the parking lot of Eagle's HQ, JC remembered his first meeting with Dr. Whitaker on this issue about 4 weeks ago. Dr. Whitaker had asked, "How is this possible? We were expecting the opposite—i.e., greater satisfaction from our MDs. Surely, they must be happy that their patients no longer complain about waiting too long to see them!" JC did not know how to respond. He told Dr. Whitaker that he will investigate.

Then, for a whole week, JC interviewed MDs to figure out what was happening. What he discovered was unexpected. MDs believed that patients were more likely to switch to another provider if their preferred care provider (PCP) did not have an open same-day appointment. They conjectured that this happened because call center employees, who booked appointments, were trained to offer a same-day appointment slot with a different MD if the patient's PCP did not have same-day availability. MDs also mentioned that Eagle had heavily advertised the availability of same-day appointments. So, patients expected to be offered a same-day appointment and often insisted on it.

JC wondered why MDs cared if patients did not make appointments with their PCPs. Upon investigating further, he found that the reason lay in how MDs' performance and pay were calculated. New MDs were paid a combination of guaranteed pay and a productivity-based bonus. They typically had more availability (open slots) than established MDs. Established MDs were paid an amount proportional to their billings. They worried that their total pay may decline under the new appointment-booking paradigm because of greater spoilage of slots. In an effort to promote continuity of care, the health system had started using PCP match as a criterion for determining MDs' performance bonus. This also generated complaints. Some MDs were able to fill nearly all of their advance-book slots with their panel patients, resulting in high PCP match. Others were not able to do so and did not perform so well on the PCP match criterion.

Some MDs reluctantly admitted that because they were also evaluated on same-day availability, they had started to reserve a few slots (keep them open) each day for same-day appointment requests. This was not how same-day paradigm was supposed to be implemented. This practice was similar to that of reserving slots for urgent cases, but with the difference that medical urgency was no longer used as a criterion to determine who should have access to the reserved slots. Anyone who demanded a same-day appointment could have access to the reserved slots if needed. As expected, the demand for same-day slots was uncertain, which meant that some slots were not filled and resulted in spoilage. To make matters worse, MDs had no guidelines suggesting how many slots should be reserved. So, every MD used whatever number they thought appropriate, resulting in widespread differences across MDs.

Clinics also allowed patients to book in advance because not every patient was able to come to the clinic on the day they called. This was particularly true of working adults who needed time off from work, and older adults who needed a family member or friend to drive them to the clinic. Some clinic administrators worried that patients upon knowing that they could get a same-day appointment were more likely to cancel or no-show. As one manager put it "patients are no longer concerned that they will have to wait a long time to get another appointment soon, if they do not keep their earlier appointment."

These revelations were all new to JC, and he was feeling pretty good about his investigative efforts when he shared these findings with Dr. Whitaker a week ago. Dr. Whitaker did not seem impressed. She wondered if MDs' and clinic managers' claims could be confirmed by the data. She said, "Surely we did not spend millions of dollars on an EMR system if we are not able to learn how same-day appointments paradigm has affected CoC and spoilage." The EMR system recorded time stamps of all patient interactions with the health system. JC remembered that there was no such data from the time prior to EMR installation. He responded, "Dr. Whitaker, I believe what you ask will be difficult, if not impossible. We do not have data from the time prior to our switch to the same-day appointments paradigm." Dr. Whitaker, a no nonsense and highly decorated doctor with more than 30 years of experience, replied, "I want answers, not excuses. Go find some hard facts."

That was a week ago. JC had several meetings with Jason, who had extracted data from multiple representative clinics and created a clean data set. This alone took several days. The data fields in the cleaned and ready-to-use data set are shown in Table 14.1. There had not been enough time to put together insights from his preliminary analysis. This was going to be an uncomfortable meeting because JC was not sure how Dr. Whitaker would react. Walking into the HQ that morning, JC was full of apprehension.

Table 14.1 Data fields—Eagle Health (A)

Name	Description
index	Index of the row
book-date-month	Month of the booking
book-date-day	Day of the booking
book-day	Day of the week when a patient calls to book an appointment
book-hr	Hour of the booking
book-mm	Minutes of the booking
appt-leadtime	Leadtime: difference between day of booking and day of appointment
appt-date-month	Month of the actual appointment
appt-date-day	Day of the actual appointment
appt-day	Day of the week on which the appointment occurred
appt-hr	Hour of the appointment
appt-mm	Minutes of the appointment
account-no	Number of the account for charging
age-cat	Age category of the patient
status	Status of the appointment
pcp-type	Type of PCP (MD, NP, other)
provider-type	Type of the provider (MD)
provider	ID of the provider
pcp	ID of the PCP
pat-id	ID of the patient
appt-day-count	Tracks the appointment day
book-day-count	Tracks the booking day
appt-scheduled-length	Scheduled length of appointment
actual-appt-length	Actual length of appointment

Chapter 15
Prime Health Partners, Inc.

The ensuing business case is written for the sole purpose of enhancing student learning via classroom discussion. It does not reflect the operations of a real health system. Any resemblance to a real health system is entirely coincidental.

It was raining hard that morning in Austin. Jay was staring out of his office window, but the rain hardly registered. His attention was entirely focused on trying to figure out what he will say to the operating room (OR) management committee tomorrow. The committee consisted of representatives from pre-op area, OR nurses, transport, post anesthesia care units, and surgeons. It had been formulated to create a sense of shared destiny among stakeholders.

Prime Health operated a medium-sized surgical hospital in Austin. The city economy was good and Prime Health was having trouble keeping up with the demand for its services. The hospital had 38 operating rooms and performed more than 17,000 surgical procedures annually. About 2 weeks ago, Steve Kumar, the hospital's COO and a mild-mannered mid-westerner who had built a reputation for achieving operational excellence in his previous stints at several hospitals, had called Jay and asked Jay to look into something that was bothering him. Jay had worked at Prime Health for more than a decade and he prided himself on having a finger on the pulse of the hospital. Still, he was caught by surprise when Steve informed him that the preoperative (pre-op) area was experiencing excessive delays.

A typical process flow diagram for patients needing surgery is shown in Fig. 11.1. Every patient scheduled for surgery undergoes a series of pre-op process steps before being wheeled into the operating room. These steps consist of change of clothing, measuring height, weight, and vital signs, recording medical history, giving any required medications through intravenous (IV) methods and visits from the patient's Surgeon, Anesthesiologist, and Certified Registered Nurse Anesthetist (CRNA). It is very important to complete all pre-op processes on time in order to not delay the case start time. Surgeons liked to start their cases early in the morning and preferred all cases to be scheduled back to back. The 7–8 a.m. surgery start time was in high demand, and most ORs were busy at that time. The ORs were scheduled

D. Gupta, *Healthcare Analytics*, Springer Texts in Business and Economics,
https://doi.org/10.1007/978-3-032-24835-0_15

to run 8 hours. Although some ORs required overtime, most ORs were done before the end of the shift.

When Steve informed Jay of the problem, Jay asked for some time to obtain data and investigate. That was two weeks ago. In the interim, Jay had obtained time stamp data and performed some preliminary analysis. He found that only 30% of the surgeries actually started on time. This did not compare well with the industry standard of 80% on-time completion of pre-op processes. The OR manager was also receiving complaints from surgeons that their cases were being delayed. Surgeons pointed the finger at the pre-op processes.

Steve had asked Jay to investigate and present his findings to the OR management committee. Jay agreed with Steve that data could help reveal the drivers of delays in surgery start times. He could think of a whole host of possible reasons—room not being ready, transport delays, surgeons being late, and a variety of logistical issues like not having the right instruments or the right staff available to start the surgery on time. However, without empirical evidence, he could not say which factors contributed the most to surgery delays. Jay desperately wanted to impress Steve. He wondered if there were some low-hanging fruit that might help him develop an action plan that could help achieve on-time completion of pre-op process for a majority of patients. He had spent a week analyzing data from the past 11 months, which contained the data fields shown in Table 15.1. However, he did not yet have a definitive answer.

Jay had taken a 2-week bootcamp on healthcare analytics with R. He remembered his instructor telling him "Every piece of data has a story hidden behind it. It is our job as analysts to bring it to light." He realized at that moment that it will be a long day and that he will be working late. He got himself a strong brew, called his wife to inform her that he will be late coming home, and sat down to start typing a R script.

Exercises

- Calculate what percentage of surgeries actually start on time?
- Are the delays occurring in the pre-op area?
- What are the key drivers of pre-op delays?
- What are some low-hanging fruit that might help Jay impress Steve?
- What should Jay do next?

Table 15.1 Data fields—Prime Health Partners

Name	Description
n_day	Day index
Sequence number	The order in which cases were scheduled
DoW	Day of week
Arrival	Patient arrival time (registration desk)
In Waiting	Patient is in waiting for pre-op
In Pre-Op	The time when the patient was taken into the pre-op area
IV Start	The time when IV was started
Pre Anesth Complete	The time when anesthesiologist visit was completed
Pre CRNA Complete	The time when CRNA visit was completed
Pre Nurse Complete	The visit with the RN was completed
Pre Circ Complete	The visit with OR nurse was completed
Pre Proc Complete	A pre-surgery procedure was completed
Out Pre-Op	Wheels out of pre-op
Actual Set Up Start	OR set up start time
OR Ready	OR ready for the patient
In OR	Patient in OR
Out OR	Patient wheeled out of OR
Start time	Surgery start time
Sched in time	Scheduled in-OR time for the patient
Total PreOp min	Total time in pre-op
Total Min OR	Total time in OR
Room	Operating room number
Service	Surgical service (department)
Primary Surgeon ID	Surgeon ID
Primary Procedure	Procedure description
Patient Class	Patient admit status
Anes	Type of anesthesia used during the procedure

Chapter 16
Sun City General Hospital

The ensuing case is written for the sole purpose of enhancing student learning via classroom discussion. It does not reflect the operations of a real health system. Any resemblance to a real health system is entirely coincidental.

Located in a mid-size rural town in northern Arizona, Sun City attracted patients from a large geographical area, being the only full-service hospital for a large swath of land. The hospital had 160 beds and 10 operating rooms. It provided a whole host of surgical services. The operating rooms (ORs) were staffed every day for 600 minutes each. The hospital employed enough core staff to open up to 10 ORs on any given day. The actual number of open ORs varied depending on the need (which depended on surgery bookings) and staff availability (which varied due to vacations and time-off requests for educational purposes). Surgeons were not employees of the hospital and billed directly for their services. Virtually, all surgeons were assigned blocks. These were periods of guaranteed OR-time allocations. Such allocations did not guarantee surgeons' access to a particular OR. The hospital had a centralized case scheduling station, where it scheduled cases one at a time. Scheduled case lengths were recommended by software that used the average of recent similar cases performed by the surgeon. Surgeons could request more than the recommended time, but not less, depending on patient characteristics.

Although many surgeons' cases on any given day were scheduled back to back in a single OR, it was not possible to schedule all cases in a single OR. This happened because some surgeries required special equipment, which was available only in some ORs. The hospital experienced both staffed OR idle time and overtime, often on the same day. The VP of operations was concerned that ORs were not scheduled optimally. De-identified surgery scheduling data fields are described in Table 16.1.

Exercises

1. Is the hospital doing a good job of estimating surgical case lengths?
2. How many ORs are open on average during normal weekday business hours?

D. Gupta, *Healthcare Analytics*, Springer Texts in Business and Economics,
https://doi.org/10.1007/978-3-032-24835-0_16

Table 16.1 Data fields—Sun City Hospital

Name	Description
seqday_book	Sequential index of day on which surgery was booked
seqday_sch	Sequential index of day for which surgery was scheduled
ormins_sch	Scheduled OR time (in minutes)
room	The OR number in which surgery was booked (from 1 to 10)
ormins_actual	Actual surgery duration (in minutes)
wkday	Day of week (1 = Monday, 5 = Friday)
mcaseno	The case number of the surgery for each room and day of surgery
mcases	Number of cases scheduled in each room for day of surgery
lastcase	A binary indicator, equal to 1 if the case was the last case for that room and day
mstart_hr	The hour at which the case was scheduled to start
mstart_min	The minute at which the case was scheduled to start
mend_hr	The hour at which the case was scheduled to end
mend_min	The minute at which the case was scheduled to end

3. What is the average and the standard deviation of the utilization of each OR during the normal weekday business hours?
4. What is the average weekday overtime usage for each OR?
5. Plot the distribution of scheduled start and close times of ORs? What does this plot tell you about the current scheduling practices?
6. Does the hospital open an optimal number of staffed ORs each weekday?

Chapter 17
Eagle Health (B)

This case is written for the sole purpose of enhancing student learning via classroom discussion. It does not reflect the operations of a real health system. Any resemblance to a real health system is entirely coincidental.

The board members were worried upon learning that the nurses' union was about to call for strike action against the management of Eagle Premier, the flagship 450-bed hospital in the Eagle Health family. A strike action will erode Eagle's market share and reputation in the community. The management had worked hard to create an environment of trust between the nurses and the management. Nurses' major complaint was that the staffing level was not adequate and that their workload was not sustainable. The board members agreed that it was necessary to gather empirical evidence because the Senior Nurse Manager assured the board that the number of nurses was more than adequate according to the nurse-to-patient targets agreed upon with the nurses' union. The hospital did not have in-house expertise in analytics.

One of the board members was close friends with Dr. Debra Goodheart (Dr. DG to her friends), a senior health consultant who worked for a top management consulting firm. He offered to ask his friend to help out, provided the board agreed to share historical administrative data for this purpose. Everyone immediately agreed that this would be a good idea.

Background

Dr. DG decided to concentrate on a cohort of six step-down units. She gathered the following background information. Eagle Premier operates six step-down units and multiple other specialized units. The step-down units also care for observational patients from the emergency department (ED). Observational patients are those patients who require a period of observation and additional tests before their diagnoses may be finalized by ED physicians. Their length of stay in the step-down unit is typically short. The hospital operates three 8-hour shifts: day, evening, and night. The day shift starts at 7 a.m., whereas the evening night shifts start at 3 p.m. and 11 p.m., respectively.

D. Gupta, *Healthcare Analytics*, Springer Texts in Business and Economics,
https://doi.org/10.1007/978-3-032-24835-0_17

Three units, labeled A, B, and C, are on one floor, and each has a 22-bed capacity. The other three units are on a different floor, labeled D, E, and F. Units D and E have 25 beds, whereas unit F has 17 beds. Unit F is not kept open all the time. It is opened when the other five units approach their full capacity. Each time it is opened, it may remain open for several days until patients recover enough to be discharged or transferred to other units in the hospital, at which time it is closed until the next demand surge. Patient transfers among these units are possible but discouraged. That being said, when transfers are necessary, it is easier to transfer patients from one unit to another if they are on the same floor. Each unit has its dedicated cohort of nurses, and some nurses may circulate from one unit to another. Typically, these nurses are senior nurses who have worked with nurses in other units in the past.

Dr. DG collected the following historical data for the purpose of her analysis. All data were provided after Dr. DG executed a nondisclosure agreement.

Data Description

Two R Data files are provided. The data files are called IPUCensusData.RData and IPUShiftsData.RData. Data fields in the first file are "dayofyear," "month," "dayofmonth," "weekday," "unit," "hour," "startingcensus," "a," "tin," "tout," "d," and "weekdayhour." Some of these data fields are self-explanatory. Definitions of some other fields are provided below (Table 17.1).

Data fields in the Shifts Data file concern the actual number of shifts worked data in units A through C. The data files are: "Shift," "unitname," "shiftcount," "Day," "Month," "dayofyear," "weekday." Note that some shift counts are fractional. This happens for two reasons: (i) Sometimes nurses are permitted to leave before their shifts end to take care of personal matters, resulting in a fractional shift to be charged to that unit's budget. (ii) Sometimes nurses are shared between units, resulting in fractional charge. The nurse that is shared circulates between the units that share the nurse.

For requirements planning, the hospital tried to maintain a N:P ratio of 1:3 during day and evening shifts on weekdays, and 1:4 on weekend and night shifts. These ratios assumed average acuity level of patients for the units concerned. It was difficult to assign fractional number of registered nurses (RNs) to a unit at planning

Table 17.1 Data fields and definitions—Eagle Health (B)

Name	Definitions
Hour	Hour of the day; 0 = midnight to 1 a.m., 1 = 1 a.m. to 2 a.m., ...
StartingCensus	Starting census in the unit (same as midnight census when hour = 0)
A	Number of admissions during the hour
T-in	Number of transfers-in during the hour
T-out	Number of transfers-out during the hour
D	Number of discharges during the hour
unit	The unit label (A, B, $\cdots$, F)

stage.[1] Therefore, the number of nurses was fixed at 7 during day and evening shifts M-F if the census was anywhere between 22 and 19 in unit labeled A through C. This number was bumped to eight nurses if there were several high-acuity patients in the unit—usually overflow from ICUs that required 1:2 or sometimes 1:1 nurse-to-patient care ratios. In addition to the RNs, the hospital provided 3 nursing assistants (NAs) if census was at or above 19 and 2 if census fell below 19 in units A through C. The unit coordinator[2] (also an RN) was tasked with developing a staffing plan for each census level and shift type. A common high-census staffing plan called for either 8/7/5 or 7/7/5 RNs during D/E/N shifts M-F and 5 nurses during weekends. Similar high-census plans for units D and E called for 9/9/6 nurses during D/E/N shifts M-F and 6 during weekends. For unit F, similar plans called for 6/6/4 nurses.

Nurses also took care of admissions, transfers, and discharges, which added to their workload. Nurses suggested that it took 2 hours to complete either an admission or discharge, and 1 hour to complete a transfer (either in or out of the unit). Therefore, they argued that the N:P ratios did not reflect their workload even when the N:P ratios were adjusted for patient acuity.

Preliminary Findings

Dr. DG quickly found that the hospital faced two major challenges. First, many of its ED physicians complain that they were unable to place observational patients into the step-down units, especially during the night shift. This resulted in ED being overcrowded and increased the likelihood of ambulance diversions and patients leaving without being seen (LWBS). Second, the hospital administration looked at average nurse-to-patient ratios to ascertain if the staffing levels were adequate. The hospital incurred significant overtime and contingent staffing costs—approximately 20% of the regular staffing costs in the previous year. These factors contributed to the management's opinion that staffing was adequate. At the same time, nurses complained that taking care of admissions, transfers (in or out), and discharges took a significant amount of time, which was not accounted for in the N:P ratio calculations.

After spending 2 days analyzing the data, Dr. DG believes she has found the root cause of the problem and calls a meeting of the board.

Exercises

- Why do nurses complain about being overworked? In particular, how do the target and realized nurse-to-patient ratio compare across different shifts? What kind of analysis might help you to identify the root cause of nurses' dissatisfaction?

[1] Note that some nurses could be shared among units, especially when they were on the same floor based on realized census and patient acuity.

[2] The unit coordinator is not counted in the nurse count for each shift, although the coordinator typically cared for one patient during day/evening (D/E) shifts and two patients during night (N) and weekend shifts.

- How will you determine the target staffing level for each unit based on historical census and ADT data?
- What are the benefits of developing staffing targets based on virtual pooling for the three units on the same floor?
- Develop a methodology to quantify the impact of recommended target staffing levels on the number of nurse shifts in excess and short, and the total staffing cost.

Appendix A
Technical Notes

A.1 The Newsvendor Model

What Is the Newsvendor Model? Health services managers often face situations in which they have to choose a quantity, e.g., the optimal number of surgical packs to have available, the optimal staffed operating room (OR) minutes, the optimal length of primary care appointments, and the optimal number of nurses in inpatient units. In all these applications, the following common features are encountered:

1. The actual demand is uncertain at the time when quantity decision needs to be made. For example, hospital managers do not know the actual demand for surgical packs on a given day, the actual number of OR minutes needed to complete all surgeries, the actual amount of time it will take a medical doctor (MD) to provide in-office consult, and the inpatient unit census, which largely determines the nurse staffing needs.
2. The health service organization incurs a cost of not having enough quantity of interest when demand does materialize. For example, if there are not enough surgical packs available, then staff have to be sent to the sterilization area to find the precise surgical tools that the surgeon needs. This takes staff time and delays surgeries, adding costs. As an exercise, please write the costs of not having enough quantity of interest in the following examples:
   - Staffed OR Minutes: ______________________________
   - Appointment Lengths: ______________________________
   - Nurses Requirements: ______________________________
3. The health service organization incurs a cost of having too much of the quantity of interest, if demand turns out to be low. For example, if too many surgical packs are made available, then some of them may need to be sterilized even though they were not used, incurring the cost of unnecessary sterilization. As an

D. Gupta, *Healthcare Analytics*, Springer Texts in Business and Economics,
https://doi.org/10.1007/978-3-032-24835-0

exercise, please write the costs of having too much of the quantity of interest in the following examples:

- Staffed OR Minutes: ________________________________
- Appointment Lengths: ________________________________
- Nurses Requirements: ________________________________

The Newsvendor model is a mathematical model that allows us to calculate the "optimal" value of the quantity of interest with minimal effort.

How Does the Newsvendor Model Work? Suppose that we face a problem in which all of the above features are present. The question we want to answer is the following: "What is the optimal value of the quantity of interest?" In order to answer this question, we need to collect the following information:

1. The distribution of demand. In particular, we need the cumulative distribution function (CDF) of demand. Let the letter D denote demand, and $F(\cdot)$ denote the CDF of demand. Then,

$$\text{Prob}(\text{D} \leq \text{x}) = F(x), \qquad \text{for any } x.$$

   In nearly all of the examples we encounter in healthcare management, x is nonnegative, i.e., $x \geq 0$. Also, usually there is a maximum possible value of D. Because $F(x)$ calculates a probability, it must lie in the interval $[0, 1]$. That is $0 \leq F(x) \leq 1$ for all values of x. Furthermore, $F(x)$ is nondecreasing because it calculates "cumulative" probability.
2. The cost of having too much of the quantity of interest. We call this c_o, or the overage cost.

   Example A hospital decides to outsource the preparation of meals. The caterer who supplies these meals often does not have enough time to prepare all of the meals after knowing demand for each day. If the meal is prepared in advance, it costs \$5 per meal. If it is prepared after learning demand, expedited processing pushes the cost to \$7 per meal. Extra meals prepared in advance are donated to a local soup kitchen for free.

   In this case, the overage cost is \$5 because an unused prepared meal is wasted.
3. The cost of having too little quantity of interest. We call this c_u, or the underage cost.

   Example Continuing with the above example, if we have too few prepared meals, then we have to pay \$7, instead of the \$5 that we would have paid to prepare it in advance. That is, the net cost of not having enough is \$7 − \$5 = \$2.

As an exercise, write down how you would calculate overage and underage costs in the following instances of the Newsvendor model:

- Staffed OR Minutes:
  - Underage Cost = ________________________________
  - Overage Cost = ________________________________

- Appointment Lengths:
  - Underage Cost = ______________________________
  - Overage Cost = ______________________________
- Nurse Requirements:
  - Underage Cost = ______________________________
  - Overage Cost = ______________________________

If we can obtain the abovementioned information, then the optimal quantity of interest can be calculated from the following formula:

$$q^* = F^{-1}\left(\frac{c_u}{c_u + c_o}\right). \tag{A.1}$$

Note that $F^{-1}(\cdot)$ is the inverse CDF function. Another way to write the above equation is as follows: $q^* : F(q^*) = (\frac{c_u}{c_u+c_o})$. The ratio $(\frac{c_u}{c_u+c_o})$ is known as the critical ratio or CR. If D is discrete, the function $F(\cdot)$ will be a step function. In that case, choose the smallest value of demand D such that the CDF corresponding to that value is either equal to or more than the CR.

In many practical situations, the health services manager may not be able to estimate c_o and c_u, *but they may be able to specify a desired demand coverage level. That is precisely the CR.*

Why Does the Newsvendor Model Work? [This section is optional. You may skip it without affecting your ability to understand what follows.]

Let us assume for a moment that we know demand, and that it is d. Then, if the health service organization chooses q as the quantity of interest, what will be its cost? It turns out that we can write this down as follows:

$$C(q, d) = c_o(q - d)^+ + c_u(d - q)^+. \tag{A.2}$$

In the above expression, we use the fact that c_o is incurred over the amount of unused quantity and c_u is paid only on the amount by which the selected quantity is short of the demand. The excess quantity is the positive part of $(q - d)$ and the shortage is the positive part of $(d - q)$, which are written, respectively, as $(q - d)^+$ and $(d - q)^+$. In reality, the health services manager does not know d. Hence, they try to minimize the expected cost, which is denoted as $\bar{C}(q) = E[C(q, D)] = c_o E[(q - d)^+] + c_u E[(d - q)^+]$. Note that we take expectation over the random demand D. In order to find the optimal q, we take the derivative of $\bar{C}(q)$ with respect to q and equate that to zero. This results in Eq. (A.1). It can be confirmed that $\bar{C}(q)$ is convex in q. Therefore, expression (A.1) returns the quantity that minimizes the expected cost.

Intuitive Explanation The optimal q^* balances the marginal cost of underage and the marginal cost of overage. The underage cost is incurred when demand exceeds q, the chosen quantity. Therefore, marginal cost of shortage $= c_u \text{Prob}(D > q) = c_u(1 - F(q))$. Similarly, the marginal cost of overage is $= c_o \text{Prob}(D \leq q) = c_o F(q)$. Upon equating the two and solving, we get Eq. (A.1).

Examples There are numerous applications of the Newsvendor model in healthcare operations management. Three such examples are provided below. *Note that in each of the potential application described below, the Newsvendor model is an approximate model. A good analyst must recognize the assumptions needed to fit the Newsvendor model to the real problem and use appropriate caution when using the result obtained from the model.*

Example A.1 A hospital administrator needs to decide how many nursing uniforms to order for the next quarter. New uniforms are issued to all new hires and to each employee once every year. In addition, some uniforms get particularly soiled and need to be replaced from time to time during the year. The administrator estimates that the demand for uniforms may be anywhere between 120 and 190 (with equal probability). Leftover uniforms are given away to staff on a first-come, first-served basis and represent a net extra cost to the hospital. Any shortage is met by placing an expedited order that costs \$50 per uniform, as opposed to the cost of bulk order of approximately \$32 per uniform. What is the optimal number of uniforms that the administrator should order.

Answer The optimal number of uniforms to order is 145. The solution is worked out below.

Here is what we know.

- Discrete demand in the interval [120, 190]. This implies that $\text{Prob}(D \leq 120 + j) = F(120 + j) = (j + 1)/71$, for any j such that $0 \leq j \leq 70$.
- Overage cost $= c_o = 32 =$ the bulk cost of the uniform if it is given away.
- Underage cost $= c_u = 50 - 32 = 18 =$ extra cost of the uniform if it is procured on an expedited basis.

Therefore, the CR is $\frac{18}{18+32} = 0.36$. From the Newsvendor model formula, we are looking for the smallest quantile either equal to or greater than 0.36. In order to solve this, we first assume that the number of uniforms need not be discrete and let $q^* = 120 + j^*$ denote the optimal number of uniforms. Then, we need to solve for

$$F(q^*) = 0.36 \tag{A.3}$$

$$\Leftrightarrow \frac{(j^* + 1)}{71} = 0.36 \tag{A.4}$$

$$\Leftrightarrow j^* = 24.56. \tag{A.5}$$

Because uniforms may be ordered only in integer quantity, we will round this up to 25, meaning the number of uniforms ordered will be $120 + 25 = 145$. The reason why we do not round to the nearest integer is that rounding j^* to 24 will not satisfy the optimality criterion.

Example A.2 A healthcare analyst hired by a primary care clinic is tasked with finding the optimal length of appointment slots. The analyst obtains historical data from past appointments and finds that actual appointment lengths are approximately exponentially distributed with parameter m such that the average appointment length equals $1/m = 20$ minutes. It was difficult to get agreement on the consequences of not scheduling enough time, although MDs agreed that they would strongly prefer not to have excessive wait between appointments. After conducting a few interviews, the analyst concludes that the cost of having shorter than needed appointment slots, which results in patient waiting, could be reasonably estimated to be 3/4 of the cost of idling the doctors. What should the clinic recommend to the clinic manager?

Answer The optimal appointment slot length is 12 minutes. However, many clinics would use 15 minutes in such cases. Therefore, the analyst should recommend 15 minutes. The solution is worked out below.

Here is what we know.

- $\text{Prob}(T \leq t) = F(t) = 1 - e^{-mt}$, for any $t \geq 0$, where T denotes the random duration of an arbitrary appointment. We also know that $m = 1/20$.
- Let the cost of overage $c_o = 1$. Then, the cost of underage, i.e., cost of having a shorter than needed appointment slot $= c_u = 3/4$.
- Critical ratio $= \frac{0.75}{1.75} = 0.43$.

Let t^* denote the optimal appointment slot length. Then, we need to solve the following equation:

$$F(t^*) = 1 - e^{-t^*/20} = 0.43 \tag{A.6}$$

$$\Leftrightarrow e^{-t^*/20} = 0.57 \tag{A.7}$$

$$\Leftrightarrow t^* = -\ln(0.57) * 20 \tag{A.8}$$

$$= 11.19. \tag{A.9}$$

From above calculations, the optimal appointment length is 12 minutes. However, in such cases, the clinic would round this number to 15. Therefore, the analyst should recommend 15-minute long appointment slots.

Example A.3 A health unit coordinator (HUC), i.e., a nurse in charge of an inpatient unit, is concerned that her unit has too many days when there are not enough nurses to take care of patients and still remain within the target nurse to patient ratio. Nurses in the unit have been complaining. Nurse shifts are 8 hours long.

The HUC approaches you for help. You obtain historical census data, and using target nurse to patient ratios, convert the raw census into a count of nurses needed to take care of patients who were admitted to the unit. Then, you try fitting different distributions to the required nurse counts each day and find that the daily nurse requirements are approximately normally distributed with a mean of 24 and a standard deviation of 4. You then go about gathering information about nursing cost and find that a full shift of a nurse, which is the amount that they work each day, costs about \$320, whereas the average cost of hiring a nurse in overtime is approximately \$600. What is the optimal number of nurses that HUC should plan to have on duty on a daily basis?

Answer The optimal number of nurses is 72. This assumes that only an integer number of nurses may be scheduled to be on duty in any shift of the day. The solution is worked out below.

Here is what we know.

- $\text{Prob}(D \leq x) = F(x)$. D is normal with mean $\mu = 24$, and standard deviation $\sigma = 4$.
- The cost of each extra nurse (overage) $= c_o = \$320$. The cost of underage, i.e., the extra cost of hiring nurses in overtime $= c_u = 600 - 320 = \$280$.
- Critical ratio $= \frac{280}{600} = 0.467$.

Let x^* denote the optimal number of nurses to hire. Then, we need to solve the following equation:

$$x^* = \text{qnorm(0.467,mean = 24, sd =4,lower.tail = TRUE)} \tag{A.10}$$

$$= 23.67. \tag{A.11}$$

Note that you may specify the qnorm function in a simpler form as follows: qnorm(0.467, 24, 4, lower.tail = TRUE). That is, you do not have to state what is the mean and what is the standard deviation, but it helps to remember.

You should recommend that the HUC hire $24 \times 3 = 72$ nurses. This comes from the fact that each nurse works 8 hours and provides 1/3 of a day's coverage.

A.2 Queueing Models For Healthcare

What Is Queueing Theory? Queues form when entities that request service, typically *patients*, arrive at a *service facility* and cannot be served immediately upon arrival. Entities that request service are not restricted to be patients, and we refer to them as *customers*, in general. Typical healthcare facilities are outpatient clinics, diagnostic imaging centers, laboratory services, and hospitals. There are also many atypical examples of customers and service facilities, as shown below.

A service facility may consist of one or more service stations where customers are served. Further, each service station may consist of one or more servers. For example, the processing of diagnostic images may require two types of servers—radiologists who read the images and transcribers who input radiologists' dictated

Customers	Service facility
Diagnostic images	Radiology department
Doctors' notes	Coding department (for billing purposes)
Prescriptions	Mail-order pharmacy
Transplant candidates	Organ procurement organization

notes into patient charts. Servers are often grouped by their expertise to form service stations, although other configurations (e.g., multiple specialty teams of doctors and nurses) are also prevalent. A common feature of the vast majority of queueing models is that servers are discrete and the number of customers waiting in the service facility are integer valued.

Queues are ubiquitous in healthcare delivery systems. Queues are also undesirable because delay in receiving needed services can cause prolonged discomfort and economic loss when patients are unable to work and possible worsening of their medical conditions that can increase subsequent treatment costs and poor health outcomes. In extreme cases, long queues can delay diagnosis and/or treatment to the extent that death occurs while a patient waits. For example, there is a severe shortage of organs in the United States, and many patients die while waiting for suitable organs for transplant.

Given the negative consequences of queues in healthcare delivery systems, the following questions naturally arise. Why do queues form? Why must customers wait to be served? Which features of system design affect queueing and by how much? What trade-offs must be considered by a service system architect when choosing system parameters? Such questions may be answered by utilizing results from a branch of mathematics called "queueing theory."

Consider a service system with an arbitrary number of stations, an arbitrary number and configuration of servers at each station, customer classes, service protocols, and sizes of waiting rooms. We treat the entire system as a black box. An arrival to this system is either turned away on account of a full waiting room, or the arrival enters the system. The stream of arrivals that enter the queueing system is characterized by arrival times $a_1 \leq a_2 \leq \cdots \leq a_j \leq \cdots$, where a_j denotes the arrival epoch of the j-th arrival in sequence, and corresponding service times $(s_1, \cdots, s_j, \cdots)$. Each customer is served either as soon as it arrives, or according to some service protocol. Given this basic setup, queueing models are frequently used to characterize the following stochastic processes:

$$L_q(t) = \text{number of customers in queue at epoch } t, \text{ and} \tag{A.12}$$

$$L(t) = \text{number of customers in the queueing system at epoch } t. \tag{A.13}$$

Clearly, $L(t) = L_q(t)+$ the number of customers receiving service at time t. Similarly, for the j-th customer, the quantities of interest are

$$W_{q,j} = \text{time in queue of the } j\text{-th customer, and} \tag{A.14}$$

$$W_j = W_{q,j} + S_j = \text{time in system (total delay) of the } j\text{-th customer.} \qquad \text{(A.15)}$$

Note that S_j in the above expression denotes the random service time of the j-th customer. For queueing systems with finite waiting rooms, we are also interested in the probability that an arrival is turned away. The purpose of mathematical models of queues is to obtain closed-form or recursive formulae that allow system designers to calculate performance metrics such as average queue length, average waiting time, and the proportion of customers turned away. In the vast majority of cases, we are able to calculate these performance metrics only in the steady state, i.e., after the queueing system has been in operation a long time. Specifically, steady-state analogs of $L_q(t)$, $L(t)$, $W_{q,j}$, and W_j are obtained when either $t \to \infty$ or $j \to \infty$ and the limiting random variables exist.

Many healthcare facilities, such as outpatient clinics, are open for a fixed amount of time during the day and experience time varying customer arrival patterns. Emergency departments, on the other hand, have demand that varies by the time of day, day of week, and month to month. In such instances, a steady state may not exist. Still, analysis of steady-state behavior can provide useful guidelines for making operational decisions.

Which Queueing Models Do I Need to Know? We will study three basic models of queues involving single servers, infinite waiting room, first-in-first-out service protocol, and independent and identically distributed inter-arrival and service times. Let $E[L_q]$, $E[L]$, $E[W_q]$, and $E[W]$ denote the steady-state average values of number in the queue, total number in service, waiting time, and total time in the system of an arbitrary customer in a queueing system. Then, the first important formula you should know, which is known as the Little's law, is the following relationship:

$$E[L] = \lambda E[W] \qquad \text{or} \qquad \text{(A.16)}$$

$$E[L_q] = \lambda E[W_q]. \qquad \text{(A.17)}$$

The second important queueing model is a single server queue with independent inter-arrival times that follow an arbitrary distribution with squared coefficient of variation C_a^2, independent and arbitrarily distributed service times with squared coefficient of variation C_s^2, first-in-first-out service protocol, and infinite waiting room. For this model, the average number in the system and the average total delay are given by the following approximate formulae:

$$E[L] \approx \left(\frac{\rho^2(1+C_s^2)}{1+\rho^2 C_s^2}\right)\left(\frac{C_a^2+\rho^2 C_s^2}{2(1-\rho)}\right) + \rho \qquad \text{(A.18)}$$

$$E[W] = E[L]/\lambda, \qquad \text{(A.19)}$$

where

$$
\begin{aligned}
E[L] &= \text{average number in system} \\
E[W] &= \text{average time in system} \\
C_a^2, C_s^2 &= \text{squared coefficient of variation} \\
&= \text{variance/mean}^2 \text{of inter-arrival and service times, respectively} \\
\rho &= \lambda/\mu = \text{utilization} \\
\lambda &= \text{average arrival rate} \\
\mu &= \text{average service rate.}
\end{aligned}
$$

Similarly,

$$
\begin{aligned}
E[L_q] &= E[L] - \rho \\
&\approx \left(\frac{\rho^2(1 + C_s^2)}{1 + \rho^2 C_s^2}\right)\left(\frac{C_a^2 + \rho^2 C_s^2}{2(1 - \rho)}\right) \qquad \text{(A.20)} \\
E[W_q] &= E[L_q]/\lambda. \qquad \text{(A.21)}
\end{aligned}
$$

There are some special cases of the above model that arise frequently in healthcare applications. For example, the scheduled service times in primary care clinics are constant (equal to the slot length). This means that $C_s^2 = 0$, and in that case, we can simplify the above expression as follows:

$$
E[L] \text{ with constant service times} \approx \left(\frac{\rho^2 C_a^2}{2(1 - \rho)}\right) + \rho. \qquad \text{(A.22)}
$$

Another special case arises when the count of arrivals in a unit interval of time follows a Poisson Distribution. When that happens, the inter-arrival times are exponentially distributed and $C_a^2 = 1$. Furthermore, if service times are also exponentially distributed, i.e., $C_s^2 = 1$ as well, and we obtain the following simpler form:

$$
E[L] \text{ with exponential inter-arrival and service times} = \left(\frac{\rho^2}{1 - \rho}\right) + \rho. \qquad \text{(A.23)}
$$

Note that I have used "=" rather than "≈" in the above expression. That is because the above expression is no longer an approximation when the inter-arrival and service times are exponentially distributed.

The third important model returns the probability distribution of waiting times and time in system when the queueing system consists of a single server with exponential inter-arrival and service times, first-in-first-out service protocol, and infinite waiting room. In particular,

$$\text{Prob}(W \le x) = 1 - e^{-\mu(1-\rho)x}. \tag{A.24}$$

Similarly,

$$\text{Prob}(W_q \le x) = 1 - \rho e^{-\mu(1-\rho)x}. \tag{A.25}$$

Insights from the Models Some immediate consequences of the models presented above are as follows: As an exercise, see if you can argue why these are true.

1. $E[L_q]$, $E[L]$, $E[W_q]$, and $E[W]$ increase as ρ increases. In fact, these quantities $\to \infty$ when $\rho > 1$. In all the models we consider, $\rho \le 1$ is strictly enforced.
2. $E[L_q]$, $E[L]$, $E[W_q]$, and $E[W]$ increase in C_s^2 and C_a^2. That is, greater variability of service and inter-arrival time causes the waiting times and numbers in the queue to increase.
3. The parameters ρ and (C_s^2, C_a^2) interact and intensify each other's effect on $E[L_q]$, $E[L]$, $E[W_q]$, and $E[W]$.

That is, queues form because either the service capacity is close to the customer arrival rate, or inter-arrival and service times are variable, and these two sets of factors interact to intensify each other's effect.

Examples The abovementioned queueing models are used in numerous healthcare applications. We provide three examples from bed occupancy calculations, panel size determination, and ED staffing requirements prediction. *Note that in each of the potential application described below, the selected queueing model is an approximate model. A good analyst must recognize the assumptions needed to fit the queueing model to the real problem and use appropriate caution when interpreting the results obtained from the model.*

Example A.4 Suppose that an emergency department (ED) of a hospital receives on average 50 new patients in each 24-hour period. Of the 50 patients, 22 are discharged after examination and treatment in the ED. The remaining 28 are admitted to the hospital as inpatients for further observation and treatment. The average length of inpatient stay is 3 days. How many inpatient beds does the hospital need to serve patients that are admitted via the ED?

Answer The Little's law allows us to estimate that on average 84 inpatient beds would be needed to serve the needs of patients that are admitted via the ED. This comes from observing that $E[W] = 3$ days, $\lambda = 28$ inpatients per day, and therefore $E[L] = \lambda E[W] = 84$. Very few assumptions are made when arriving at this result. For example, Little's law remains valid regardless of the priority of service of arriving patients and differences in their service times in the ED.

Example A.5 A primary clinic manager has ascertained, using historical data, that in that clinic, the expected number of appointment requests per day per panel patient is approximately 0.02. She is interested in estimating target panel size for MDs who work two 4-hour sessions a day with a total of 16 appointment slots per day. The clinic manager has decided to choose panel sizes such that no more than 8% of the patients need to wait more than 6 days for an appointment. What is the target panel size?

Answer The target panel size is 800. Here is what we know.

- Unit of time = 1 day.
- Service rate = μ = 16 patients/day.
- We need to find λ, the arrival rate of appointment requests.

$$\text{The maximum Prob(W} > 6\text{)} = e^{-\mu(1-\rho)\times 6} = 0.08$$

$$\iff -6(16 - \lambda) = \ln(0.08)$$

$$\iff \text{The maximum } \lambda = 16 + \frac{\ln(0.08)}{6} = 15.579.$$

Finally, the desired panel size, $N = \frac{15.579}{0.02} = 778.95$. The clinic manager will likely round this number to 800 for ease of implementation.

Example A.6 Recall that in a single-server queue, the customers' average wait time can be calculated from the following approximate formulae:

$$E[L_q] \approx \left(\frac{\rho^2(1 + C_s^2)}{1 + \rho^2 C_s^2}\right)\left(\frac{C_a^2 + \rho^2 C_s^2}{2(1 - \rho)}\right) \tag{A.26}$$

$$E[W_q] = E[L_q]/\lambda, \tag{A.27}$$

where

$$E[L_q] = \text{average number in the queue (also called backlog)}$$

$$E[W_q] = \text{average waiting time}$$

$$C_a^2 = \text{squared coefficient of variation of inter-arrival times}$$

$$C_s^2 = \text{squared coefficient of variation of service times}$$

$$\rho = \lambda/\mu = \text{utilization.}$$

You obtain data from an ED during its busy period. Each of these data is calculated on a per-hour basis.

Patient arrival rate	5 per hour
Number of MDs available	3
Service rate of each MD	1.8 per hour
C_a^2	0.8
C_s^2	1

Assume that no one leaves without being seen. (i) What is the average number of patients waiting in the ED waiting area during its peak period? (ii) On average, how long do patients wait to be seen by an MD?

Answer (i) $L_q = 10.33$ and (ii) $W_q = 2.07$ hours. Here is what we know.

- $\lambda = 5$.
- $\mu = 3 \times 1.8 = 5.4$.
- $\rho = \lambda/\mu = 0.926$.
- It is good to note that $\rho < 1$. If not, you may argue that number of patients waiting and waiting times will go to infinity.
- Because $C_a^2 = 0.8$ and $C_s^2 = 1$, we get

$$E[L_q] \approx \left(\frac{\rho^2}{1+\rho^2}\right)\left(\frac{0.8+\rho^2}{1-\rho}\right).$$

Because we know ρ, we solve for $E[L_q]$ to obtain $E[L_q] = 10.33$ and $E[W_q] = 2.07$ hours.

A.3 The Linear Programming Model

What Is Linear Programming? Numerous business situations require managers to make decisions that affect their firm's costs or profits. The managers choose values of decision variables under constraints. Common constraints are resource and budget constraints, whereas common decision variables are the optimal quantities of different types of products and services the firm should produce. Linear programming is a mathematical model that casts such problems into a standard format and utilizes powerful algorithms developed by researchers to solve for the decision variables. Such situations arise frequently in healthcare management as well. Common features of linear programs are as follows:

1. A set of n decision variables, often denoted as $x_1, x_2, \cdots, x_n$, where n depends on the problem context. In many cases, we use two subscripts because that makes it more convenient to write down the objective function. For example, $x_{i,j}$ may denote the decision to either assign surgical case i to OR j or not. In such cases, the number of decision variables is equal to the product of the possible values of index i and index j. For example, if we have to decide which cases to assign to which ORs, and there are 32 cases and 10 ORs, then there would be 320 decision variables.
2. A set of costs or revenues associated with each choice of x_i. These are called coefficients of the objective function and their values are known. Let us denote such coefficients by $c_1, c_2, \cdots, c_n$. Note that the objective must be a *linear* function of x_is.
3. A set of *linear* resource or budget constraints. Suppose the number of such constraints is m. Then, the i-th constraint is of typically written as follows:

$$a_{i,1}x_1 + a_{i,2}x_2 + \cdots + a_{i,n}x_n \leq b_i.$$

The values of $a_{i,1}, a_{i,2}, \cdots, a_{i,n}$, and b_i are known for each $i = 1, \cdots, m$.

4. A set of constraints that specify whether the decision variables are nonnegative, or binary, or integer.

Putting this all together, a typical linear program has the following structure:

$$\min_{\{x_1,\cdots,x_n\}} \; c_1x_1 + c_2x_2 \cdots + c_nx_n$$

subject to

$$\begin{aligned} a_{11}x_1 + a_{12}x_2 + \cdots + a_{1n}x_n &\leq b_1 \\ a_{21}x_1 + a_{22}x_2 + \cdots + a_{2n}x_n &\leq b_2 \\ &\vdots \\ a_{m1}x_1 + a_{m2}x_2 + \cdots + a_{mn}x_n &\leq b_m \\ x_i &\geq 0 \qquad \text{for every } i. \end{aligned}$$

The matrix of coefficients of the constraints

$$\begin{bmatrix} a_{11} & a_{12} & \cdots & a_{1n} \\ a_{21} & a_{22} & \cdots & a_{2n} \\ \vdots & \vdots & & \vdots \\ a_{m1} & a_{m2} & \cdots & a_{mn} \end{bmatrix}$$

is known as the coefficient matrix.

How Does the Linear Programming Model Work? The first algorithm to solve a linear program, known as the simplex method is now more than 50 years old. In the last 15 years, tremendous progress has been made in refining solution algorithms for linear programs, with the result that modern solvers can handle large-scale problems with thousands of constraints and variables. Many solvers can also handle binary and integer decision variables, although in such cases the solver may return near optimal solution, rather than the guaranteed optimal solution.

Solvers require users to specify the problem in a standard format. This format consists of the vector of coefficients of the objective function, the coefficient matrix, and the vector of right-hand side values. Finally, the user must also specify the sign of each constraint (i.e., whether it is a "$\leq$" or a "$\geq$" constraint), whether the objective is to minimize or maximize the objective function, and non-negativity or binary variable requirements. Two of the most powerful commercial solvers are CPLEX and Gurobi.

Examples There are literally an uncountable number of applications of linear programming in healthcare operations management. Two such examples are provided below. *Note that in each of the potential application described below, the linear programming model is an approximate model of the reality. A good analyst must recognize the assumptions needed to fit the linear programming model to the real problem, and use appropriate caution when using the result obtained from the model.*

Example A.7 A laboratory that specializes in nonstandard tests is planning to offer standard diagnostic tests to regional hospitals. These tests can be performed by available staff, analyzers, and materials. The lab manager has assessed the following requirements for each test:

Test type	A	B	C	D	E	Available resources
Profit/test ($)	8	10	8	7	10	
Staff (minutes/test)	15	15	15	20	25	3400 mins
Analyzer (minutes/test)	20	40	40	60	45	6000 mins
Materials (ml/test)	12	15	16	14	14	2800 mls

How many tests of each type should the lab perform in order to maximize its profit?

Answer In order to answer the question, we cast the problem as a linear program. The objective is to maximize profit. Because we need to decide how many tests of each type to perform, the decision variables may be written as follows:

- x_i = number of type i tests performed, where $i \in \{A, B, C, D, E\}$.

Then, the objective function is $8x_A + 10x_B + 8x_C + 7x_D + 10x_E$, which the lab manager would like to maximize by choosing x_is.

The constraints come from limits on available staff and analyzer time, and available materials. Because there are three types of resources, there are three constraints. These may be written as follows:

$$15x_A + 15x_B + 15x_C + 20x_D + 25x_E \leq 3400$$

$$20x_A + 40x_B + 40x_C + 60x_D + 45x_E \leq 6000$$

$$12x_A + 15x_B + 16x_C + 14x_D + 14x_E \leq 2800$$

Finally, the number of tests performed cannot be negative. Therefore, we have the following non-negativity constraints:

$$x_i \geq 0 \qquad \text{for every } i \in \{A, B, C, D, E\}.$$

Caution *In reality, x_is must be integer valued. We ignore that constraint in the above formulation because x_is are expected to be large and rounding down will produce a feasible integer valued solution, which will be very close to the optimal integer-valued solution.*

See if you can guess the number of constraints in the above formulation.

Example A.8 Thousands of individuals with end-stage renal disease (ESRD) are currently on waiting lists for deceased-donor kidneys. The supply of kidneys is much smaller than the demand. In order to pair donors with recipients, various tests are performed to determine the compatibility (tissue, blood type, antigens, etc.), which for our purpose is described by a match score. The match score can range from 1 to 6, with 6 denoting perfect match. The table below denotes the match score for six potential recipients and four potential donors. What is an optimal allocation of donor organs to recipients if the goal is to maximize the total match score?

Match Scores

	Recipients					
Donors	R1	R2	R3	R4	R5	R6
D1	1	6	1	2	4	2
D2	4	5	1	3	1	2
D3	6	1	2	3	3	5
D4	3	4	5	6	2	2

Answer The decision variables are as follows:

$$x_{ij} = \begin{cases} 1 \text{ if donor } i \text{ is assigned to recipient } j \\ 0 \text{ otherwise.} \end{cases}$$

Note that $i \in \{1, 2, 3, 4\}$ and $j \in \{1, 2, \cdots, 6\}$. That is, in this problem setting, there are 24 decision variables.

The objective function may be written as

$$\sum_{i=1}^{4} \sum_{j=1}^{6} p_{ij} x_{ij},$$

where p_{ij} = match score when donor i is paired with recipient j. The constraints are of the following type:

- A donor may be paired with at most one recipient.
- A recipient may be paired with at most one donor.
- x_{ij} are binary (only 0 or 1).

These constraints can be written as follows:

First type of constraints (four of these):

$$x_{1,1} + x_{1,2} + \cdots + x_{1,6} \leq 1$$

Second type of constraints (six of these):

$$x_{1,1} + x_{2,1} + \cdots + x_{4,1} \leq 1$$

And, finally, we have

$$x_{ij} \in \{0, 1\}.$$

Now we can solve this problem using lpsolve function in R. The optimal total match score is 21. Here is a sample R code. It uses a coefficient matrix file. The coefficient matrix for this example is also printed below.

```
# Install package lpsolve
install.packages("lpSolve",repos = "http://cran.us.r-project.org")
library("lpSolve")
# Import the csv file containing the coeff matrix
coeff_matrix <- read.csv('organ.csv')
coeff_matrix[is.na(coeff_matrix)] <- 0

# Set the objective function. These are the donor-recipient match
scores f.obj <- c(1, 6, 1, 2, 4, 2, 4, 5, 1, 3, 1, 2, 6, 1, 2, 3, 3,
5, 3, 4, 5, 6, 2, 2)

# Set the constraints. Notice that since we have the coeff_matrix
ready, we simply assign this matrix to the constraints
f.con <- coeff_matrix
# Set the direction of the constraints. All 10 constraints are <=
constraints f.dir <- c(rep("<=", 10))

# Set the RHS of the constraints. The RHS is 1 for all constraints.
f.rhs <- c(rep(1,10))
# Run the LP
lp ("max", f.obj, f.con, f.dir, f.rhs, binary.vec=1:24)
# Output the solution
lp ("max", f.obj, f.con, f.dir, f.rhs, binary.vec=1:24)$solution
```

Coefficient Matrix

x_{11}	x_{12}	x_{13}	x_{14}	x_{15}	x_{16}	x_{21}	x_{22}	x_{23}	x_{24}	x_{25}	x_{26}	x_{31}	x_{32}	x_{33}	x_{34}	x_{35}	x_{36}	x_{41}	x_{42}	x_{43}	x_{44}	x_{45}	x_{46}
1	1	1	1	1	1	0	0	0	0	0	0	0	0	0	0	0	0	0	0	0	0	0	0
0	0	0	0	0	0	1	1	1	1	1	1	0	0	0	0	0	0	0	0	0	0	0	0
0	0	0	0	0	0	0	0	0	0	0	0	1	1	1	1	1	1	0	0	0	0	0	0
0	0	0	0	0	0	0	0	0	0	0	0	0	0	0	0	0	0	1	1	1	1	1	1
1	0	0	0	0	0	1	0	0	0	0	0	1	0	0	0	0	0	1	0	0	0	0	0
0	1	0	0	0	0	0	1	0	0	0	0	0	1	0	0	0	0	0	1	0	0	0	0
0	0	1	0	0	0	0	0	1	0	0	0	0	0	1	0	0	0	0	0	1	0	0	0
0	0	0	1	0	0	0	0	0	1	0	0	0	0	0	1	0	0	0	0	0	1	0	0
0	0	0	0	1	0	0	0	0	0	1	0	0	0	0	0	1	0	0	0	0	0	1	0
0	0	0	0	0	1	0	0	0	0	0	1	0	0	0	0	0	1	0	0	0	0	0	1

References

Arrow, K. J. (1963) Uncertainty and the welfare economics of medical care. *The American Economic Review, 53*(5), 941–973.
Committee on Quality of Health Care in America and Institute of Medicine (2001). *Crossing the quality chasm*. National Academies Press.
Gupta, D., & Potthoff, S. J. (2016). Matching supply and demand for hospital services. *Foundations and Trends®in Technology, Information and Operations Management 8*(3–4), 131–274.
Gupta, D., et al. (2006). Performance metrics for advancede access. *Journal of Healthcare Management, 51*(4), 246–58. Discussion 258–9.
Gupta, D., & Wang, W.-Y. (2012). Patient appointments in ambulatory care. In R. Hall (Ed.), *Handbook of healthcare system scheduling*. International series in operations research & management science (Vol. 168, pp. 65–104). Springer.
Jayakumar, P., et al. (2019). Integrated practice units: What are they and how can they be applied to orthopaedic trauma? *Journal of Orthopaedic Trauma, 33*(Suppl 7), S43–S48.
James, B. C., & Poulsen, G. P. (2016). The case for capitation. *Harvard Business Review, 94*(7–8), 102–11, 134.
Little, J. D. C. (1961). A proof for the queuing formula: $L = \lambda W$. *Operations Research, 9*(3), 383–387. https://doi.org/10.1287/opre.9.3.383
Murray, M., & Berwick, D. M. (2003). Advanced access: reducing waiting and delays in primary care.*JAMA 289*(8), 1035–1040.
Porter, M. E., & Kaplan, R. S. (2016). How to pay for health care. *Harvard Business Review, 94*(7–8), 88–98, 100, 134
Song, Z., et al. (2019). Health care spending, utilization, and quality 8 years into global payment. *New England Journal of Medicine 381*(3), 252–263. https://doi.org/10.1056/NEJMsa1813621

D. Gupta, *Healthcare Analytics*, Springer Texts in Business and Economics,
https://doi.org/10.1007/978-3-032-24835-0

Index

D. Gupta, *Healthcare Analytics*, Springer Texts in Business and Economics,
https://doi.org/10.1007/978-3-032-24835-0

MIX
Papier aus verantwortungsvollen Quellen
Paper from responsible sources
FSC® C105338

If you have any concerns about our products,
you can contact us on
ProductSafety@springernature.com

In case Publisher is established outside the EU,
the EU authorized representative is:
Springer Nature Customer Service Center GmbH
Europaplatz 3, 69115 Heidelberg, Germany

Printed by Libri Plureos GmbH
in Hamburg, Germany